MURDER, MICHIGAN

**Seventy fascinating and dramatic murders
that have violently shaped
the dark side of Michigan history**

GARY W. BARFKNECHT

Author of *MICHILLANEOUS*

Friede Publications

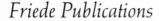

Friede Publications
510 North Lapeer Street
Davison, Michigan 48423

Printed in the United States of America

ISBN 0-9608588-1-4

To

Tom Powers

and all my other friends

at the

Flint Public Library

CONTENTS

INTRODUCTION

Most of us think that murders take place on the fringes, or even outside, of other historical events. To most of us, murders are random, unthinkable acts that are committed somewhere in the dim haze surrounding "normal" events, "normal" life, and "normal" history.

But the dramatic act of murder, like any other historical event, requires a time and a setting. At any point in Michigan's past, the conflicts, political atmosphere, physical environment, technical progress, economic conditions, and all the other ingredients and forces that combine to define a date or era in history also provide a unique opportunity to murder and need only intersect with someone with the desire to kill.

This book, then, is a history book, an exploration of the dark side of Michigan's history from before the white man until the present. Most murders in this book were selected because the participants, murderers and victims alike, are swept, almost helplessly, to their violent, irretrievable destiny by historical forces. Other murders are included because their details dramatically and colorfully illustrate a moment, time, or era in Michigan's history. And, finally, murders which did take place on the fringes or outside other historical events are included because they are so sensational, brutal, or unusual, that they have left their own indelible mark on Michigan's or the nation's history.

Murder, Michigan does not claim, by any means, to be a comprehensive, all-inclusive catalogue of all, or even many, of the murders that have been committed in Michigan. Unfortunately, so many murders have taken place throughout Michigan's history (currently at the rate of approximately 900 each year) that such a work would be encyclopedic in length.

Nor do all the killings detailed in *Murder, Michigan* necessarily fall under the strict legal definition of murder which, though it changes from time to time and place to place, basically is the unlawful, willing, intentional killing of another human being by a sane adult person. The killings in *Murder, Michigan,* whether or not they fit the legal or dictionary definition of murder, do all, with one exception, involve the grisly spectacle of one human being willfully depriving another of his or her right to live.

WHAT IS A
CHIPPEWA LIFE WORTH?

Straits of Mackinac
June, 1567

At the very least, they demanded, one Ottawa brave should die.

Oeunas, a young Ottawa brave, carefully checked his shell-tipped spear, bone hooks, and the new fishing net his squaw had made from pieces of twisted bark, then eagerly set out for his favorite fishing spot. After spending another harsh winter in their crude, cold, and smoky bark-covered lodges, Oeunas, his squaw, and twenty-four other families, as similar Ottawa bands had done for centuries, followed the spring thaws north to the Straits of Mackinac. After months of eating venison jerky, Oeunas and the other men looked forward to netting, hooking, and spearing whitefish, perch, herring, and sturgeon and hunting small game while the elders, women, and children gathered nuts, berries, and honey.

Across the Straits' cold, gray, choppy water, Oeunas could see the lodges, fires, and large canoes of the Chippewas dotting the shore. Though Oeunas had never met a Chippewa, he had learned from his elders that they spoke the same language. The Great Spirit, said the elders, had put a family of "Three Fires," Ottawa, Chippewa, and Potawatomi, along the great lake as its caretaker. The Chippewa were the eldest brother in their family and a younger brother, the Potawatomi, camped many days farther south along the eastern shore of the great lake.

The three brothers spoke the same language and lived in peace without formal borders or treaties. If the ancient Indians had ever passed along the true story of their arrival in Michigan, that story had, over the centuries, become lost in the simple legend of the "Three Fires."

In probable fact, not legend, the ancestors of the "Three Fires" first set foot on the North American continent about fourteen thousand years ago when, during the Ice Age, sea levels dropped drastically and, at the Bering Straits near Alaska, frozen land bridges formed between Asia and North America. At that time, small bands of Indians, similar to modern Eskimos, crossed the 56-mile gap and, over the next twelve thousand years, wandered throughout North America including Michigan.

In Michigan, shortly before the voyage of Columbus, a once united group split into several tribes, the largest and most dominant being the "Three Fires" — the Ottawa, Chippewa, and Potawatomi. The Ottawa lived in the northern Lower Peninsula, the Chippewa roamed the Upper Peninsula, and the Potawatomi farmed along the eastern shore of southern Lake Michigan. At the Straits of Mackinac, the informal border of the Chippewa and Ottawa territories, the two tribes had lived harmoniously for more than a century, trading goods, occasionally intermarrying, and sharing hunting and fishing territory.

Oeunas, however, did not like the idea of sharing and jealously guarded the location of his secret fishing spot even from members of his own band. Three summers earlier, he had discovered a hidden stream that emptied into the Straits and had cast tobacco onto the waters as a gift for Nanabozho, the Spirit of the Fish. Nanabozho had been pleased with the tobacco, thought Oeunas, for the spirit had blessed him with bountiful catches, and the young brave had received great honors from his band for the full nets of fish he brought back each day.

But, as Oeunas stepped quickly along the familiar, smooth, gray stones that marked the final ten feet through the brush to his secluded waterway, he came face to face with a Chippewa brave who had paddled across the Straits and placed his nets in the same fish-filled stream.

Startled and shocked, Oeunas sternly blurted, "I am an Ottawa brave who has fished these waters for three summers and I would like you to remove your nets."

The Chippewa stood erect and replied, "The waters of the Great Spirit belong to all men. I will take the fish as I please."

Oeunas, enraged at this unexpected challenge, lunged forward, pulled his crude antler dagger from his breechcloth, and plunged the bone shaft deep into the surprised Chippewa's heart. The Chippewa fisherman jerked straight, stared blankly into Oeunas' eyes for a few seconds, then, as gushing blood clouded the clear water, fell lifelessly into the stream.

The Chippewa and Ottawa elders and chiefs had never had to deal with such an act. Murder within their own tribes was extremely rare, and never had a member of one tribe killed a member of the other.

The elders and chiefs held many councils, gave many speeches, and smoked many pipes of tobacco. The code of both tribes dictated that every deed, good or bad, toward another person be balanced by an equal and fair act in return. Under this code, they had always traded goods fairly and honestly. Six Chippewa deerskins were worth one Ottawa knife; but what was a Chippewa life worth? The Chippewas threatened bloodshed and war as revenge for the murder. At the very least, they demanded, one Ottawa brave, preferably Oeunas, should die.

But an Ottawa elder replied, "We are here to confess to you the crime committed by one of our young men upon your brave. Our nation does not approve of the murder. You know that we are brothers of the fire, that your ancestors and ours have long smoked the calumet (peace pipe) together, and that our dead are in the other world, in the same place as yours. We cannot, then, permit one such act of murder to break the union which our ancestors had with you, and which we have maintained. We have, therefore, come with the design of averting your resentment."

The Ottawa chiefs and elders then offered the entire Leelanau Peninsula to the Chippewas as well as granting them unlimited access to all the rivers and streams in the Lower Peninsula to trap beaver, mink, otter, and muskrat. The Chippewas accepted and Indian justice was served.

THE ANNIHILATION OF THE MUSH-QUAH-TAS

Emmet County
August, 1598

The beautiful young maiden pulled a robe against her naked body and peacefully bowed her head to the fatal blow.

Twelve Ottawas, returning from an attack against the Sac Indians, paddled their canoes toward a tiny Mush-quah-ta village lying on the Lake Michigan shoreline near (present-day) Seven-Mile Point in Emmet County. The brave and warlike Ottawas, long at peace with their Michigan neighbors, the Chippewa, Potawatomi, and smaller tribes like the Mush-quah-ta, gratified their thirst for battle by frequently raiding distant tribes such as the Wisconsin Sacs.

In this most recent battle, the Sacs had killed five Ottawas, and the bodies lay in the canoes as the surviving braves headed toward shore. As they neared the Mush-quah-ta village, the Ottawas chanted and wailed woefully for their dead comrades and, as was the proper Indian custom, expected the Mush-quah-tas to join in their mourning.

But the Mush-quah-tas, an intelligent, industrious, and peace-loving tribe, had long harbored a deep contempt for the aggressive Ottawas and their warlike expeditions. That contempt boiled to the surface, and when the Ottawas' canoes touched the beach, the young men and boys of the village pelted the Ottawa warriors with balls of ashes wrapped in forest leaves while chanting, "Killers!" and "Bloodthirsty savages!"

Shocked, hurt, and deeply insulted, the Ottawas quickly left, returned to their own village, and told their proud people about the grave insult. The Ottawa chiefs called a joint council with their Chippewa allies and friends, and, together, they decided that only Mush-quah-ta blood could avenge such an insult.

Several days later, on a calm, warm, August night, the Mush-quah-tas slumbered peacefully as the faint, glimmering light in the east revealed shadowy figures slinking through the cornfields toward their village. A long line of Ottawa braves approached from one side and the Chippewas from the other, moving so quietly that even the Mush-quah-tas' watchful dogs weren't alarmed. Hundreds of the shadowy forms entered the village and crouched in front of the Mush-quah-ta lodges.

Suddenly, with a deafening, blood-curdling chorus of furious yells, the attackers threw open the wigwam doors and mercilessly attacked the occupants. In one lodge, an old brave reached for his war club and feebly raised it in defense, but an Ottawa crushed his skull with one tomahawk blow. A young brave in the next lodge reached for his bow, but two Chippewas killed and scalped him before he could reach an arrow. A beautiful young maiden pulled a robe against her naked body and peacefully bowed her head to a fatal blow. A mother fought furiously to protect the life of her infant, but two attackers held her while a third picked up her baby by its feet and smashed it against the ground several times. The two then stabbed the mother in the chest and the third threw the baby's bleeding and lifeless body upon its mother's red bosom.

When the sun rose, all but one of the Mush-quah-tas lay dead on the bloody ground or had been incinerated in burning wigwams. The Ottawas' revenge was complete.

LOVE SLAVE

Sault Ste. Marie
October, 1619

My wife will not be happy with your presence in our lodge.

Kota, a plump, homely, orphaned Chippewa maiden from a band near (present-day) L'Anse, fell madly in love with Shahgo, a handsome, young Chippewa brave who had come to the area from (present-day) Sault Ste. Marie to hunt during the winter. Kota aggressively pursued Shahgo and told him quite bluntly that she would like to return to the Sault with him as his wife. But Shahgo, a courteous and mild-mannered brave, tactfully explained that he had, only a year earlier, already married and was not interested in taking a second wife.

"But, Shahgo," Kota relentlessly argued, "you know that the law of our Chippewa nation allows a man to have more than one wife. And you know that when a man marries, even for the second time, it must be to a woman from a band not his own."

For a moment, Shahgo, who was not accustomed to arguing with women, could not think of a reply. He certainly knew that, to strengthen the blood ties among the Chippewa nation, all Chippewa marriages took place between members of different bands. And he also knew that, though a man could marry more than one woman, not many did because it caused too many problems. A man's first squaw, though required and allowed to do only menial and tedious tasks, had absolute control of her lodge and everything in it. If a second wife entered the lodge, she became the property of the first wife and subject to her control. So Shahgo finally replied, "My wife, Peewahsheek, is a very strong and jealous woman. She would not be happy with your presence in her lodge."

If that argument was supposed to discourage Kota, it didn't, and she followed the reluctant and frustrated hunter back to his summer lodge near the Sault. Shahgo sheepishly approached his lodge, greeted his wife, Peewahsheek, and tried to explain Kota's presence. But, before he finished, Peewahsheek shrieked in anger and jealousy, picked up a large stick of firewood, and chased the fat, frightened girl into the forest.

For days, Kota sat in the woods surrounding the camp, staring forlornly at Shahgo and begging Peewahsheek to allow her into the lodge. "Please," she asked, "allow me to be your slave. I will carry wood and water. I will not lie with Shahgo but will lie at your feet at night. I will do anything just to be in the same lodge as Shahgo."

After three weeks of the constant pleading, Peewahsheek concluded that Kota would not leave unless forced. So, determined to drive the love-sick girl away with cruelty and abuse, Peewahsheek took Kota into her lodge as a slave. During the hot summer months, Peewahsheek, while reclining in listless idleness in the cool shelter of her bark wigwam, threw sticks and stones at Kota and called her names while the slave dressed game, cured skins, ground corn, gathered wood, and twisted bark into rope. But, in spite of the constant indignities and cruelties, Kota showed no sign of leaving.

By October, Peewahsheek could not stand the sight of Kota any longer. Shahgo would soon leave for the L'Anse hunting grounds, and, thought Peewahsheek as Kota entered the lodge with an armful of wood, this relentless, obnoxious woman would probably ask Shahgo to bring her along so she could visit her former band. If they were together all winter who knows what might happen, worried Peewahsheek. So, as Kota knelt to place the wood in the corner, Peewahsheek grabbed her husband's tomahawk in both hands, raised it high over her head, and, with a blow powered by months of anger and jealousy, crushed Kota's head. Peewahsheek then dragged Kota's body outside and ordered her surprised husband to dispose of it.

Since Peewahsheek was mistress of her lodge, the outsider's murder didn't particularly upset or concern anyone in Shahgo's band. And, since Kota had no relatives in her distant band, no one demanded justice and Peewahsheek escaped punishment.

THE MURDER OF MICHIGAN'S FIRST WHITE VISITOR

New York State
1632

As a beginning to what they had planned as a slow and agonizing death, the Indians took turns pulling out handfuls of Brule's beard.

As Shahgo's wife plunged her tomahawk into the head of her rival, Etienne Brule, a young French explorer, paddled his canoe along the rocky north shore of Georgian Bay on a route that, in one year, would lead him to Shahgo's village and, in thirteen years, to a violent death.

Nearly a hundred years earlier, France, Europe's wealthiest and most populous nation, had begun a serious search for the fabled "Northwest Passage," a short cut to the spice-rich Orient. From 1523 to 1608, French navigators explored the North American coastline from Virginia to Newfoundland, entered the Gulf of St. Lawrence, and made their way inland to Montreal.

In 1608, Samuel de Champlain, lieutenant governor of "New France," brought 16-year-old Etienne Brule with him to Quebec and sent him and other French explorers deep into the surrounding unexplored wilderness. Brule eagerly plunged into the interior, spent a year living with the Huron Indians, and learned their language and customs. Brule loved this life and, upon his return to

Quebec, begged Champlain to let him push even farther west.

Still hoping to discover a water route to the Pacific, Champlain agreed, and Brule and a companion, Grenoble, set their canoes in the eastern waters of Georgian Bay, paddled along the rocky north shore, and, in 1620, entered the island-strewn St. Mary's River near Shahgo's village. Pushing on against the current, they finally reached the rapids where Lake Superior water tumbles down over the rocks on its way to Lake Huron. As Etienne Brule stepped out of his canoe to view the rapids, he became the first white man to set foot on Michigan soil. Brule and Grenoble then paddled along the south shore of Lake Superior, passed through the copper country, and eventually reached as far west as (present-day) Duluth, Minnesota.

Brule returned to Quebec in 1623, reported his findings to Champlain, and, anxious to return to the wilderness and Indian life, went back into Canadian Huron country, turned southeast, and made his way into upstate New York. There, a party of Iroquois captured Brule and, as a beginning to what they planned as a slow and agonizing death, took turns pulling out handfuls of his beard. Brule threatened them with the wrath of the Great Spirit, and, as though planned by a Hollywood scriptwriter or director, a thunderhead suddenly and miraculously blackened the sunny sky, boomed ominously overhead, and hurled lightning bolts at the earth. The frightened Iroquois quickly untied Brule, humbly fell to their knees, fed him a large dinner, and sent him on his way with many gifts and best wishes.

The relentless adventurer spent the next several years wandering through the wilderness, living with perhaps a hundred different Indian tribes and, eventually, becoming more Indian than white. But, in 1632, because of some unknown insult, slight, or breach of custom, the New York Hurons clubbed Michigan's first white visitor to death, boiled his body, and ate it.

ONONTIO'S BLOOD

St. Ignace
November 29, 1683

It is enough, you accuse yourselves; the French are now masters of your bodies.

Other French explorers, missionaries, and traders followed Brule to Michigan, explored the coastline, and traversed the rugged peninsulas on foot. Jean Nicolet, still searching for the fabled shortcut to the riches of the Orient, discovered the northern expanse of Lake Michigan in 1634 and followed the shore from the Straits of Mackinac to Green Bay. Seven years later, two Jesuit missionaries established a mission at Sault Ste. Marie, and, in 1668, Father Jacques Marquette founded the first permanent settlement in Michigan at that mission. From these missions and settlements, *coureurs debois*, "woods rangers," plunged into the rugged interior of the Upper Peninsula, and *voyageurs* paddled frail bark canoes hundreds of miles up the region's swift streams and across uncharted lakes.

The Jesuits pursued lost Indian souls; *coureurs debois* and *voyageurs* pursued Indian furs, and, by the 1680s, fur trading had become the backbone of New France's economy. To command and protect the important water routes that led to this great resource, the French constructed strategic forts at Sault Ste. Marie, St. Ignace, and Port Huron. French traders set out in canoes from these small, log stockade forts to Indian villages where they bartered tools, weapons, pots, blankets, and other white man's goods for Indian furs.

Two such traders, Jacques LeMaire and Colin Berthot, their large bark canoes loaded with tobacco, gunpowder, cloth, and other trade goods, left Sault Ste. Marie in late summer 1683 for a Chippewa village and major trading post at Kianon (Keweenaw Bay). Shortly before the two Frenchmen reached the post, Folle-Avoine, a hostile, murderous Ottawa, and the two eldest sons of Achiganaga, chief of a different Ottawa band, shot the two traders, brought their bodies to a marshy area, pushed them into the ooze, and piled tree branches over the corpses so they would not float to the surface during the following spring's rising waters. The murderers then hid the valuable contents of the canoe, bashed in its side, and brought it to the village. LeMaire and Berthot, they sadly reported to the eighteen Frenchmen living at the village, must have drowned in a tragic accident and all trade goods were lost.

Shortly after, however, one of Achiganaga's sons, while

under the influence of whiskey taken from the dead traders, loudly boasted about the murders and theft, and, that autumn, word of the crimes reached Daniel deGresolon Sieur duL'Hut (Duluth), commandant of Fort DeBaude at (present-day) St. Ignace. Determined to emphatically establish French law by publicly punishing Berthot's and LeMaire's murderers, Duluth ordered the arrest of Achiganaga, his sons, and Folle-Avoine.

As Duluth organized the manhunt, Folle-Avoine unintentionally delivered himself almost directly to the commandant. After murdering an Indian from another tribe, Folle-Avoine, unaware that Duluth knew of Berthot's and LeMaire's murders, had fled from Kianon to presumed safety at Sault Ste. Marie. Duluth paddled to the Sault, arrested Folle-Avoine, brought him under guard to St. Ignace, then sent a trusted lieutenant, M. Pere, and eight other men to Kianon to arrest Achiganaga and his sons.

Though Duluth commanded fewer than one hundred French soldiers in the midst of an Indian population that, in the immediate area alone, approached two thousand, he called a council of chiefs and boldly demanded, "Do not try to free the prisoner, Folle-Avoine, or I will have no choice but to punish your whole nation. I have sent soldiers to Kianon to bring back others who may have helped shed the blood of my brothers. When they return, you must help separate the guilty from the innocent." The Indians, believing that Pere and his detachment could not capture the remaining murderers, or would themselves be killed trying, slyly blamed only Achiganaga and his sons for the killings. For three days, the chiefs demanded that Duluth release Folle-Avoine, but the commandant refused.

Meanwhile, at Kianon, Achiganaga, under the pretext of defending his small band from a hostile neighboring tribe, assembled a large war party. When Pere and his soldiers saw the large, fierce-looking group, thought Achiganaga, they would quickly forget about the arrests and turn back. But Achiganaga's allies, angry that the chief had tried to dupe them into protecting murderers, helped Pere arrest Achiganaga and his children. On November 24, 1683, Pere returned to St. Ignace with the prisoners.

Duluth called another council of Indian elders and chiefs and, in their presence, interrogated the prisoners individually. Each testified that Chief Achiganaga had neither planned nor participated in the crimes, so Duluth set him free. And, though Folle-Avoine and Achiganaga's sons admitted their own involvement in the theft, each accused the others of committing the actual murders.

Seeing that the chiefs and elders were satisfied that all the prisoners had convicted themselves of murder, Duluth then offered the council the opportunity to dispense justice. Duluth expected the council to follow Indian custom and order the deaths of the three, but a council spokesman turned to the prisoners and said with contempt, "It is enough, you accuse yourselves; the French are now masters of your bodies."

"Very well," said the surprised Duluth, "I have determined that, under the law of Onontio*, all of the guilty should die. Onontio has lost blood, and it is necessary to have the blood of the guilty to satisfy him. But, following

---

*An Indian term, similar to "Great White Father," for any governor general of New France.

the Indian code of putting to death a man for a man, I will execute only two, Folle-Avoine and Achiganaga's eldest son."

On November 29, 1683, Duluth and forty-two soldiers, surrounded by four hundred murmuring Indians, raised their rifles, pointed them at the two condemned Indians, squeezed the triggers, and, under the laws of France, carried out the first legal execution in Michigan.

LET SLEEPING DOGS LIE

Detroit
June 5 and 6, 1706

The uneasy harmony quickly deteriorated, and Bourgmont's insensitivity led to two murders and at least thirty other needless deaths.

A little more than a year before the executions at St. Ignace, Sieur de LaSalle, a French explorer, reached the mouth of the Mississippi River at the Gulf of Mexico and claimed all the land in the Mississippi Valley and Great Lakes region for France. At the same time, English colonists pushed into the same territory from their east coast colonies creating a conflict that, for the next eighty years, sporadically erupted into war and violence. The French had to deal with this threat from the east, and, as the English pushed toward Michigan, Antoine de la Mothe Cadillac arrived at the mouth of the Detroit River and, on July 24, 1701, began construction of Fort Ponchartrain du Detroit to protect the strategic water route from Lake Erie to Lake Huron.

Cadillac also had great dreams of establishing a permanent settlement there, but, in spite of his elaborate efforts to attract settlers and encourage settlement, by 1707 only sixty-three permanent white residents lived at the Fort. Young Frenchmen preferred the adventure and quick profits of the fur trade to the hard toil of farming.

Indians, on the other hand, eagerly responded to Cadillac's invitations, and, by 1706, nearly two thousand Chippewas, Hurons, Ottawas, Miamis, Potawatomies, Mississaugas, Mohicans, and others had settled in small villages around the log stockade. Through Cadillac's leadership, these diverse tribes, in spite of a turbulent undercurrent of ancient jealousies and hatreds, co-existed fairly harmoniously.

But, in 1704, Cadillac was ordered back to Quebec, and, a year later, Sieur deBourgmont took command of Fort Ponchartrain. Under Bourgmont's criminally incompetent leadership, the uneasy harmony that had existed between the various Indian tribes quickly deteriorated. The most hostile feelings developed between the Ottawas and Miamis, and Bourgmont's insensitivity and gross mishandling of that conflict led to two murders and at least thirty other needless deaths.

Bourgmont committed the first murder himself. On June 5, 1706, a curious Ottawa brave peered into the doorway of the commander's headquarters. Bourgmont's startled dog bit the uninvited visitor who then reflexively kicked the animal in the ribs. As the dog yelped and cowered in a corner, Bourgmont attacked the Ottawa and beat him so severely that the Indian died. Bourgmont's insensitive murder reinforced rumors that the French had united with the Miami to destroy the Ottawas, and young Ottawa warriors angrily called for war against the Miamis and the French.

The next day, several young Ottawas hid along both sides of a path leading to a Miami village and, when a group of eight Miami elders passed between them, shot and killed seven of the unsuspecting chiefs. The whooping Ottawas then chased the lone survivor toward the French fort. Other Miamis, who were camped very near the fort, heard the gunfire and the Ottawas' furious shouts and scurried with the escaping chief into the wooden stockade. The excited Ottawas charged after them but stopped as the fort's gates closed.

Then, as the hesitant attackers milled around the fort, Bourgmont ordered his troops to fire. The soldiers' bullets killed several of the Indians, and the survivors quickly retreated.

As the sullen and beaten Ottawas made their way back to their village, they met Father Constantin D'Halle who, unaware of the battle that had taken place, was returning to the fort from his garden at St. Anne's church. The furious Indians grabbed, bound, and stabbed the surprised French *Recollect*.

The Ottawas then regrouped and, while roughly pushing the wounded priest in front of them, marched back toward the fort. As they neared the stockade, one of the chiefs ordered Fr. Constantin released, but, as the priest approached the fort's gates, an Indian killed him with a musket shot. Bourgmont again ordered his troops to fire, and they killed thirty more Ottawas.

For the next month and a half, the Ottawas hovered menacingly around the fort but finally left without any further bloodshed.

BREAK HIS HEAD
Detroit
November 7, 1707

When word reached Quebec of the violence in Detroit, the governor of New France ordered Cadillac back to Fort Ponchartrain to restore order. But by the time Cadillac arrived, Bourgmont had deserted the fort and fled with several other soldiers and civilians to Ohio.

Fifty of Cadillac's soldiers pursued the deserters and captured three. One, Bartellemy Pichon, was tried, found guilty of treason, and sentenced by Cadillac to "have his head broken 'til death follows, by eight soldiers, being first degraded of his arms."

On November 7, 1707, Cadillac's soldiers, using their rifle butts to bludgeon Pichon to death, carried out the first legal execution of a white man in Michigan.

A SAVAGE ACT

Piqua, Ohio
June, 1752

Attackers savagely ripped open the bellies of pregnant women and threw live children into blazing fires.

As English fur traders and colonists pushed closer to Michigan, they successfully competed with the French for Indian loyalty and alliance. The French, determined to continue their domination of the area, sent soldiers from Michigan into the Ohio Valley to drive out the rapidly advancing British and persuade the Indians to remain loyal to the French. Most tribes received the French with formal courtesy, but some, like Chief LaDemoiselle (or "Old British," as he was known) proudly displayed British flags and, with open, warlike hostility, proclaimed their friendship to King George.

The French, alarmed that LaDemoiselle's brash, hostile attitude might spread, set out to brutally punish him. In early June, 1752, under commission of the French government, Charles Mouet, a half-breed trader, assembled a force of 250 Ottawa and Chippewa Indians from Sault Ste. Marie, St. Ignace, and Detroit and fiercely attacked LaDemoiselle's village at (present-day) Piqua, Ohio. Attackers savagely ripped open the bellies of pregnant women, while others threw live children into blazing fires. A few grabbed children by the feet and smashed their heads on rocks before throwing the bodies into the human fires. The Michigan Indian raiders destroyed the entire village and, as a final act of savagery, carved out LaDemoiselle's heart and ate it.

Shocked and alarmed by this attack, the British rallied and, over the next eight years, slowly but determinedly drove the French back to their supply base at Quebec. In September, 1759, British General James Wolfe defeated a French force under General Louis Montcalm on the Plains of Abraham outside Quebec, and France's domination of North America ended.

When the news of the French defeat reached Fort Michilimackinac, the commandant fled. On November 29, 1760, Captain Francoise deBellestre formally surrendered Fort Ponchartrain to the British, and French rule in Michigan ended.

CLAPHAM'S LAST DRUNK

Presque Isle
July, 1762

Clapham became drunk, loud, and boisterous, unaware that his two slaves stood off to the side muttering intensely.

After winning control of North America, the British faced the problem and responsibility of dealing with the area's Indians in order to protect and govern the region's white residents. Unfortunately, the first governor general of British North America, Lord Jeffrey Amherst, totally lacked respect for Indians, whom he considered crude, uncivilized, and savage. Amherst's experienced advisors urged him to expand trade with the tribes and to continue the French policy of buying Indian friendship with lavish gifts of food, guns, ammunition, and liquor. The insensitive Amherst, however, opposed any further "coddling" of the "savages" and dictated that the Indians receive only small amounts of clothing and a few guns, but no food or alcohol.

Michigan Indians suddenly found themselves cut off from a major source of the white man's goods upon which they had come to depend, and wondered why. When no British official dared explain Amherst's disastrous policy, French traders and trappers exploited the situation by telling the Indians that the British deliberately withheld food, clothing, and guns to weaken the tribes as part of a plot to exterminate them. A burning hatred for the British smoldered just beneath the Indians' stoical surface.

In mid-summer, 1762, Clapham, an English trader operating out of Detroit, purchased two Pawnee slaves and, either unaware of or unconcerned about the Indians' growing hatred for anyone British, took the man and woman by canoe to Presque Isle. Near Presque Isle, they met five Mascouten Indians, and, as they made camp and built a fire for the night, Clapham shared his rum with his two slaves and five guests. Clapham became drunk, loud, and boisterous, unaware that his two slaves stood off to the side muttering intensely. As Clapham sat down on a log, swayed back and forth, and sang loudly, the Pawnee woman silently crept up behind him and cracked him over the head with a large rock. As the trader fell face first into the dust, the Pawnee man grabbed a razor-sharp knife from one of the Mascoutens and cut off Clapham's head. The drunk Mascoutens and slaves then divided Clapham's trade goods among themselves, dumped his body into the river, and threw his head onto the fire.

The next morning, the sober Mascoutens, regretting their part in the brutal murder, delivered the two slaves to a group of English traders who then relayed the report of the murder to Major Henry Gladwin, commandant at Fort Ponchartrain. Before Gladwin's soldiers arrived to arrest the two Pawnees, the man escaped to Illinois. But Gladwin's troops returned the woman to Detroit where she was tried, convicted, and sentenced to death.

In February, 1763, the Pawnee woman became the first woman legally executed in Michigan when she was publicly hanged in Detroit.

CANNIBALISM ALONG THE ST. CLAIR

Port Huron
May 6, 1763

Suddenly, the women and children scattered, and the Indian men, naked bodies painted red and black, charged into the water.

From sporadic, spontaneous murders like Clapham's, Michigan Indians rapidly grew more organized in violently expressing their hatred for the British. Early in the spring of 1763, a highly respected Delaware Indian called "The Prophet" preached that, because of the British and other whites, alcoholism, prostitution, and a host of other evils plagued and corrupted Indian society. Inspired by the Prophet's pleas to free themselves of British control, several bands of Huron, Potawatomi, Seneca, Delaware, and Ottawa Indians living near Detroit held war councils and plotted against the British.

Just after daybreak, May 2, 1763, Captain Charles Robertson, six soldiers, two sailors, and two English "curiosity seekers," left Fort Ponchartrain in a large bateaux and a dugout canoe and headed up the St. Clair River toward (present-day) Port Huron. The group moved steadily, passing several unusually quiet and deserted Indian villages as they took soundings to see if large sailing ships could navigate the river.

At about 8:00 a.m. on May 6, while delivering a few barrels of flour at (present-day) Marysville, Captain Robertson mentioned to the French Canadians who were building a sawmill there that all the Indians seemed to be away from their villages hunting that day. "No," said one Frenchman emphatically, "I have just returned from the distant woods where, in our cabin last night, the Indians gathered, sang their war song, and talked of taking up the hatchet against the British. The Indians have heeded the words of the Prophet and are waiting in ambush for the British, six miles up the river. If you proceed any further, you will certainly be cut to pieces. You, sir, should return to your fort immediately."

But, in spite of this direct and ominous warning, Captain Robertson ordered the party to continue up the river. Two hours later, they approached Port Huron when, suddenly seemingly out of nowhere, four hundred Indians appeared on the riverbank. Though the Indians shouted greetings and called the Englishmen "brothers," Captain Robertson ordered the crew to paddle harder against the current. But the swift current forced their vessels closer to shore, and, in spite of the crews' strongest efforts, the Indians could walk along the riverbank faster than the Englishmen could paddle. Squaws and children pressed and crowded forward, urging the English to come ashore and exchange goods. As the Indian women held out fish and maple sugar for the Englishmen to see, Indian warriors, hidden by this living, moving curtain, stripped off their blankets and ornaments and picked up weapons.

Suddenly, on a signal, the women and children scattered, and the Indian men, naked bodies painted red and black, charged into the water while firing at the eleven Englishmen. Several bullets slapped into the bodies of Robertson, two soldiers, and one of the tourists, killing them instantly. The Indians rushed forward, eager to grab a living Englishman by the hair and thus become his future master. The Indians dragged their new slaves and the dead bodies through the water to shore. There, the Indians decapitated the tourist's body, scalped all the dead men, stripped the bodies naked, and, while wearing the Englishmen's clothes, buried all the bodies except Captain Robertson's.

That evening, drunk on liquor taken from the bateaux, the Indians cut up Robertson's body, roasted it, and forced some of their captives to join them in eating it.

BLOOD SPORT

Mackinaw City
June 2, 1763

Suddenly, their sporting shouts turned to ferocious war whoops as the squaws threw open their blankets exposing guns, hatchets, and knives.

A month before the murder of Robertson and his party, Chief Pontiac, an Ottawa chief who had assumed the military leadership of the Prophet's fight against the British, called a war council of several Indian nations on the banks of the Ecorse River. There, he revealed to the gathered chiefs a sinister, rather simple, yet effective plan to capture the fort at Detroit. He and sixty of his best warriors, each concealing tomahawks, knives, and muskets, would request a parley, gain entrance to the fort, and, at a given signal, attack the surprised soldiers.

An informer, however, warned the British, and, on May 7, 1763, when Pontiac and his braves entered the fort, they were immediately surrounded by the heavily armed soldiers. After expressing indignation at the hostile attitude of the British, Pontiac and his warriors quickly left.

Pontiac failed, but others using his basic strategy succeeded. June 2, 1763, dawned hot and sultry as the soldiers inside Fort Michilimackinac prepared to celebrate King George's birthday. Outside, a small group of Chippewas approached the fort and asked the commandant if they and a team of Sacs could play a game of *boggattaway* (a combination of lacrosse and football) outside the fort in honor of the king's birthday. The commandant, ignoring the warnings of his superiors in Detroit that an Indian attack was imminent, said, "yes,' and the Indians marked off the field and set goalposts outside, but near, the fort's gates.

The Chippewas and Sacs, ready to begin their game, then invited the officers and soldiers to come outside and watch, relax, and even bet on the outcome. The commandant nodded permission, and groups of soldiers moved outside, leaving the fort's gates wide open while they stood in the shade without their guns. As sober chiefs and amused soldiers watched the game, large numbers of squaws, wrapped to the throat in blankets though the day was almost oppressively warm, gathered near the open gate. In the midst of the game, the ball fell near the fort's open gate, and the players rushed toward it.

Suddenly, their sporting shouts turned to ferocious war whoops as the squaws threw open their blankets exposing guns, hatchets, and knives. The Indians threw down their rackets, grabbed the weapons, and savagely attacked the amazed British soldiers and traders before they had time to react. One survivor later wrote: "The dead were scalped and mangled; the dying were writhing and shrieking under the unsatiated knife and tomahawk; and from the bodies of some, ripped open, their butchers were drinking the blood, scooped up in the hollow of joined hands and quaffed amid shouts of rage and victory."

The Indians killed twenty-two soldiers and traders, captured twenty others including the commander, and destroyed or carried off everything belonging to the English. None of the French families living at the fort or their property was touched.

Over the next month and a half, other Indians, using Pontiac's strategy, ravaged nine of twelve British forts throughout the East and Midwest. Then, for the next year, Indians attacked settlements from New York to Virginia, and so serious was this uprising that for a time the region west of the Appalachian Mountains was closed to settlement by royal edict.

In October, 1764, the British held a peace council with the Ottawa, Huron, Chippewa, Miami, and Potawatomi Indians which ended the greatest Indian war in American history.

DEATH PRAYER
Muskegon
Late Summer, 1809

Joseph LaFramboise, a devout Catholic, retired to his tent to pray, unaware that Nequat followed behind.

In September, 1796, Joseph LaFramboise, a professional fur trader, took sole charge of his company's western Michigan territory. Though America had won its war of independence and signed a peace treaty with England in 1783, the British had not left their Detroit and Michilimackinac forts until only a month before. Now that the British soldiers had finally gone, LaFramboise's company wanted to move quickly into British fur trading territory and gain supremacy in the Michigan fur trade.

LaFramboise had recently married Madeline Marcotte, a beautiful, refined half-breed who had been raised by the Indians and educated by the Jesuits. The couple chose a site near the rapids of the Grand River at (present-day) Ada for their winter headquarters and brought with them firearms, knives, hatchets, tobacco, liquor, silk, Irish linen, blankets, gold and silver jewelry, chocolate, and other desirable trade items. Those quality goods, Joseph's shrewdness, and Madeline's tact and intimate knowledge of Indian culture and custom quickly established them as the most successful traders of their day. Their reputation attracted even distant tribes to their post, and, when the spring sunshine broke away the

29

ice barriers, the LaFramboise bateaux rode low in the water from the weight of the furs they carried back to Mackinac Island.

During the winters at Ada and the trips to and from Mackinac, Joseph and Madeline lived primitively, as did most of the small number of whites living outside the Detroit area. Eighty percent of Michigan's four thousand white residents, though part of the new United States of America, still spoke French and lived in Detroit. The rest, mostly wandering British or French fur traders like the LaFramboises, lived along main rivers in wooden huts not much more substantial, sophisticated, or comfortable than the Indians' bark-covered lodges.

But during their summers at Mackinac Island, the central fur depot for over one hundred years, Joseph and Madeline mingled easily and comfortably with the finest society of the island.

For more than twelve years, Joseph and Madeline regularly spent comfortable summers at Mackinac and harsh, rugged, challenging winters at Ada. Even the creation of the Michigan Territory by the U.S. Congress in 1805 and a subsequent unsuccessful attempt by the American government to enter the lucrative fur trade didn't much disrupt the LaFramboises' routine and peaceful lifestyle.

But the summer of 1809, unusually cold and dreary, changed their routine, and Joseph and Madeline decided to leave Mackinac earlier than usual. They journeyed uneventfully to their last encampment near a Potawatomi village on the bluffs beyond (present-day) Muskegon. Their sworn brothers, the Potawatomi, as they had done for so many years, received the traders cordially, and, after preparing their camp for the night, Joseph shared a pipe and exchanged small talk with a group of his Indian friends.

Suddenly, Nequat, a brash young brave, walked boldly up to the group and said to Joseph, "I know you have whiskey. Give me some." Joseph, slightly taken aback, but seeing that the other Indians were also shocked by the bold request, said, "No. The whiskey must go to our post. If you would like to come there later and trade for it, you may."

Nequat glared and said, "I want whiskey. Give me some or I will take it."

Joseph stood and replied sternly, "I said 'no' and I mean no. If you try to take it, your brothers will carry you away."

Nequat took a step forward but, seeing that the other Indians were prepared to support LaFramboise, hurried away and brooded sullenly over his embarrassing challenge and retreat. From a distance, he watched resentfully as Joseph smoked pipefuls of tobacco with the other members of his tribe and Madeline entertained the squaws with descriptions of Mackinac Island society dances.

After several hours, Joseph, a devout Catholic, retired to his tent to pray, unaware that Nequat followed close behind. As Joseph kneeled to pray, Nequat silently entered the tent, tapped Joseph on the shoulder and, as the bearded trader turned toward him, crunched his dagger through Joseph's breastbone and into his heart. As Joseph clenched his fist and gurgled his last breath, Nequat fled into the dark forest.

Stunned and deeply saddened by Joseph's brutal murder, but also strong and determined, Madeline buried her husband at (present-day) Grand Haven, continued to their winter home, spent the season trading as usual, and tried to forget her tragic loss.

That spring, as Madeline prepared to return to Mackinac, a delegation of solemn Potawatomies approached the post roughly pushing Nequat, his hands tied, in front of them. All winter they had relentlessly hunted the killer of their beloved friend, Joseph LaFramboise, and now presented the murderer to the widow for judgment. A Potawatomi spokesman said, "We have brought to you, Madame LaFramboise, the wicked Indian Nequat who, in an evil moment, murdered your husband. Why he did it we do not know. In the years you have lived among us there has grown up between us a love which a Potawatomi seldom has for a white person or one partly white as you are. Your many deeds of kindness to us and honest treatment of us have prompted us to bring to you Nequat, the murderer of your beloved husband. We beg of you to state the manner in which he shall be killed as punishment for the crime he committed."

Prepared to execute Nequat immediately before Madeline's eyes, the spokesman bowed his head, paused, and waited for her to pronounce the death sentence. But to his amazement she replied, "My brothers, you have shown the love you had for my husband and the respect which you now feel for me. But through the long winter, the malice I bore the slayer of my husband has passed away. Seeking solace for the shadow that has darkened my life forever, I have read the Good Book which bids us forgive seventy times seven. I know that would be the wish of my husband were he now living. I will, therefore, forgive this captive and leave him to the Great Spirit. My desire is that you do likewise and give him his life." Reluctant and uncomprehending, the tribesmen untied Nequat, scornfully banned him from the Potawatomies forever, and sent him stumbling into the forest.

Later that summer, Nequat's maggot-covered body was found deep in the forest with his dagger plunged into his chest to the hilt. In spite of Madame LaFramboise's compassion and forgiveness, someone had avenged her husband's death.

A FATAL TWIST OF FATE
St. Joseph
June, 1812

While cocking his rifle, Jean Baptiste Chandonai said, "If you cross over the line I have just marked, you do so in peril of your life."

More than three years after the murder of her husband Joseph, word reached Madame LaFramboise and other outstate residents that, as of June 18, 1812, the United States was again at war with Great Britain. For years, while locked in a death grapple with France during the Napoleonic Wars, Britain had routinely violated the rights of neutral nations, including the United States, on the high seas. Britain's actions began to interfere with

America's commerce, and, when the British began snatching sailors from American vessels and forcing them to serve on British warships, the United States declared war.

Britain's actions on the high seas had had little effect in Michigan. However, the territory's residents, convinced that the British had been secretly arming the Indians for years to discourage settlement of the area, supported war.

Though Britain unquestionably ruled the seas, Americans knew the British would need the help of Indians to win the war on land, and Indian loyalty became a prime concern to both sides.

So, when in late June, 1812, the Potawatomies living in the (present-day) St. Joseph area scheduled an important council to decide on whose side they would fight, the British and Americans each sent a representative to try to persuade the Indians to join their side. The Americans selected Jean Baptiste Chandonai, a French half-breed, as their ambassador and, in an ironic, bizarre, and fatal twist of fate, the English sent, as their agent, his uncle, John Chandonai.

The elder Chandonai, enraged at finding his nephew there on behalf of the Americans, placed his hand on the handle of his sword and demanded that Jean Baptiste either immediately join the British cause or surrender himself prisoner.

Baptiste looked incredulously at his uncle for a moment, then scratched a line with his foot in the dirt and stepped back about five yards. While cocking his double-barreled rifle and raising it slowly he said, "Uncle, I will not abandon the American cause nor will I allow you to take me prisoner. We have come here to talk, not fight, but if you should pass over the line I have just marked, you do so in peril of your life." But John Chandonai, sensing a bluff from his young nephew, determinedly drew his sword and boldly started toward Baptiste. The instant John crossed the line, a ball from his nephew's gun exploded his heart and he fell dead.

John had brought thirty Chippewa Indians with him, and, when they saw his dead body fall into the dust, they moved threateningly toward Baptiste. Baptiste cocked the other barrel of his rifle and said, "I'm sorry I had to kill my uncle, but, had he taken me prisoner, I myself would have been killed. I would also be sorry to kill one of you, but I will if you cross the line." Baptiste then persuaded the Indians to help him bury his uncle, paid them with ten gallons of rum, and left for Detroit.

Two months later, when the British captured Detroit without firing a shot, they arrested Baptiste for murder and treason and sent him in hand and leg irons to their fort at Amherstburg, Ontario. But Baptiste escaped and fled to Chicago where he stayed until the Americans recaptured Detroit in September, 1813. On Christmas Eve, 1814, British and American negotiators signed the Treaty of Ghent, and the War of 1812 ended.

A TIME FOR REVENGE

Port Huron
Spring, 1815

To complete their revenge the Indians took Rodd's bloody coat
back to his wife and showed her the bullet holes.

During the War of 1812, most of the Indians living in
the Port Huron area declared their allegiance to the
British. But Alexander Rodd, a half-breed, rejected and
insulted the Indians by adamantly refusing to do the
same. The Indians never forgave Rodd and patiently bid-
ed their time for revenge.

The spring after the war's end, a band of Saginaw
Chippewas who had settled in Canada, paddled across
the river and asked Rodd if he would guide them on a
hunting expedition through some unfamiliar territory
west of Port Huron. Rodd, who, along with his family,
was busy making maple sugar, hesitated but, when the
Indians said they would pay him handsomely, reluctantly
agreed. The group started out along the south bank of
the Black River with Rodd in the lead and the Indians
following in single file. After walking without conversation for about five miles to (present-day) Wadhams, the
Indian immediately behind Rodd suddenly stepped out
of line to the right, and the Indian behind him shot Rodd
in the back. As Rodd lay writhing in agony in a patch of
snow, another Indian shot him in the side, and a third
stepped up and ended Rodd's thrashings by putting a
bullet through his head.

The Indians buried Rodd where he fell, and, to complete their revenge, took his bloody coat back to his wife, showed her the bullet holes, then took Rodd's entire family into captivity for a year before releasing them.

CHE-QUI-OCK

Grand Haven
Fall, 1818

They heard the distant thump of an approaching drum accompanied by the mournful voice of an Indian chanting his own death song.

The end of the War of 1812 marked the beginning of dramatic change in Michigan. The British had been driven out forever, and never again would Indians organize to fight against whites. As a result, many families who had previously avoided the Michigan Territory because of Indian and British unrest came to settle. In 1816, the government began surveying public lands. By 1817, Robert Fulton's new invention, the steamboat, traveled regularly between Buffalo and Detroit bringing new settlers to Michigan, and by 1820, Michigan's population had grown to nearly nine thousand. Most settlers poured into southeast Michigan, and by 1823, Wayne, Monroe, Macomb, Oakland, St. Clair, Lapeer, Lenawee, Sanilac, Shiawassee, and Washtenaw counties had organized.

But most of the rest of Michigan still remained rugged wilderness inhabited mainly by Indians. One of these Indians, Buhnah, had also come to Michigan as a settler. After wandering across Canada and through Minnesota, Wisconsin, and Illinois, the happy-go-lucky Indian had, in 1808, decided to settle with a Manistee tribe near (present-day) Grand Haven. The Manistee, like most Michigan Indians, had adopted white man's clothing, tools, utensils, weapons, and, unfortunately, alcohol but, at the same time, had also preserved many of their centuries-old values, customs, and their sense of justice. Buhnah faithfully followed his adopted tribe's customs and laws and even married one of their maidens.

But Buhnah was not much of a success as an Indian, and it seemed that the only luck he had was bad. A fair hunter but poor trapper, all Buhnah had to show after ten years with the Manistee were eight scruffy children, the clothes on his back, and a few traps.

The other Indian men of the village, not sharing Buhnah's blood, showed little sympathy or respect and sometimes even provoked and teased him. One evening during the fall of 1818, Taychatin, son of Manistee Chief Ahkushtish, drank whiskey with Buhnah and, during an argument, called Buhnah "an old woman and a coward." Drunk and frustrated, Buhnah jumped up, waved his knife through the air, and shouted, "You may be the chief's son, but you cannot call me an old woman. Take back your words." But Taychatin laughed and scornfully said, "Sit down, squaw, before you hurt yourself." At that remark, Buhnah wildly flailed his knife through the air and drove it into Taychatin's temple.

Instantly sobered by his bloody act, Buhnah ran to his lodge and told his wife what he had done. "I am a dead man," he said, "for I have killed Taychatin and have no worldly goods to offer Chief Ahkushtish as repayment for his son's life. My only chance at keeping my life is to flee for the winter, trap many beaver, mink, marten, and other furs, and return in the spring in the hope that these furs will appease Chief Ahtushkish.

"My husband, what you say is true," replied Buhnah's wife, "but I must remind you that, if you do not return, it is the custom of our tribe to take the life of my young brother, Kaanwi, in your place. I think you should tell him of your plans." Buhnah agreed and, after getting Kaanwi's approval and blessing, the killer and his family escaped to the marshes at the headwaters of the Muskegon River.

After burying Taychatin, Chief Ahkushtish and his remaining two sons discussed what penalty they should demand of Buhnah and, knowing that he was too poor to pay any type of restitution, demanded his death. And, since they also believed Buhnah and his family had fled permanently to Canada, they demanded, just as Buhnah's wife had said, the death of Kaanwi. But young Kaanwi explained Buhnah's plan for restitution, said he would personally go to Buhnah's hiding place in the spring, and, if he could not bring him back, would willingly offer his own life instead.

Chief Ahkushtish agreed, and, in the spring, Kaanwi made the difficult journey to the headwaters of the Muskegon River. Buhnah had fled with very little ammunition, and, by the time Kaanwi arrived, Buhnah and his family had nearly died of starvation. And, because of the unusually heavy snowfall that winter, Buhnah had trapped no marten, beaver, or mink to offer Chief Ahkushtish. So Buhnah and his family, empty-handed and downcast, stoically marched toward Grand Haven and his execution.

Soon after sunrise, the news spread through the Manistee camp that Buhnah was coming, and soon every Indian in the village heard the distant thump of an approaching drum accompanied by the mournful voice of Buhnah chanting his own death song. Chief Ahkushtish and his family hastily arranged themselves around a spot they had chosen for the execution, and Indians and white traders gathered on the surrounding hills to watch. Moments later, Buhnah, his wife, and his children slowly marched in single file into the valley.

When Buhnah reached the sitting chief, he placed his drum on the ground, and his wife and children seated themselves on mats Chief Ahkushtish's sons prepared for them. Buhnah then spoke to the chief saying, "I, in a drunken moment, stabbed your son. I fled to the marshes at the head of the Muskegon hoping that the Great Spirit would favor me in the hunt so that I could repay you for your lost son. I was not successful. Here is the knife with which I killed your son; by it I wish to die. Save my wife and children. I am done."

Chief Ahkushtish took the knife, handed it to his eldest son, and solemnly said, "Kill him." The large crowd fell silent, and only the singing of birds broke the silence as Chief Ahkushtish's eldest son stepped toward Buhnah. Buhnah's wife and children, eyes fixed upon their husband and father, sat perfectly motionless and silent. Chief Ahkushtish's son placed his left hand on Buhnah's shoulder, made two or three feints with the knife, then plunged it into Buhnah's breast to the handle and immediately withdrew it.

Buhnah stood motionless, his eyes fixed upon his executioner as he received the blow without the slightest tremor. For a few seconds, he remained erect, blood gushing from the wound at every pulsation, then his knees began to shake and he sank lifeless upon the sand. Buhnah's wife and children threw themselves upon the dead body and sobbed so sadly and uncontrollably that a murmur of sympathy ran through the crowd.

Chief Ahkushtish watched the grieving family for twenty minutes then approached Buhnah's widow and, in a trembling voice said, "Woman, stop weeping. Your husband was a brave man and, like a brave, was not afraid to die as the rule of our nation demanded. We adopt you and your children in the place of my dead son. Our lodges are open to you and you may live with any of us. We will treat you like our sons and daughters. You shall have our protection and love."

The witnessing Indians muttered among each other, "Che-qui-ock" (this is right) and the tragedy ended.

CHIEF KESHKAUKO'S LAW
Saginaw
1823

Not only did Chief Keshkauko violate the white man's law, but also murderously broke the Indian's code.

Keshkauko, chief of the Saginaw Bay Chippewas, was one of the few Michigan Indians who remained bitterly hostile to Americans after the War of 1812. Keshkauko defied American law at every opportunity, and his reputation for cruelty prevented all but the bravest whites from settling along the wilderness trail that stretched from Detroit to Saginaw. Keshkauko and a constant bodyguard of ten vicious Indians traveled this trail twice a year, entering the homes of the few whites who dared settle in his domain, beating the inhabitants, and taking anything they wanted. No one dared resist; no one dared complain to the law, for the white man's law meant nothing to Keshkauko.

Not only did Keshkauko violate the white man's law but also violently broke the Indian's code. In 1823, Keshkauko presided over the trial of a Delaware Indian who had killed one of Keshkauko's Chippewas in a drunken brawl. At the council, the dead man's relatives, as was their choice under Indian code, accepted the slayer's offer of gifts and did not demand his life. As both parties smoked the pipe of peace, Keshkauko quietly arose, stepped behind the Delaware, and drove his tomahawk into the man's head, killing him instantly.

When the stunned Indians asked Keshkauko why he had interfered with the old law, he said with savage energy, "The law is now changed."

But three years later, Keshkauko violated both the Indian and white man's law, and his reign of terror finally ended. In late summer, 1826, Keshkauko, his son Big Beaver, and several other members of his band stole some whiskey and got violently drunk while camped at a farm near Detroit. The party ended in a fight, and Keshkauko and Big Beaver hacked the head of one of the other men to pieces. When they came to town boldly carrying their bloody hatchets, they were arrested, tried, found guilty, and sentenced to be hanged. But, as Keshkauko had defied the white man's law in life, he also cheated it in death. The day before his scheduled execution, Chief Keshkauko drank poison supplied by his visiting wives, and died in his jail cell.

In spite of the Chief's violent, lawless, and murderous reputation, the state legislature, in 1840, named a newly created county "Keshkauko." Three years later, after great protest, the legislature renamed the county "Charlevoix."

BEWARE OF
STRONG DRINK

Wayne
Spring, 1830

As his terrified daughters tried to restrain him, the 250-pound man drew back his huge fist.

Following the opening of New York's Erie Canal in 1825, people from the New England area flocked to Michigan and, during the next five years, nearly tripled the territory's population to 31,000. Because of bandits who prowled the bad roads at night, most of these travelers, upon reaching Michigan, stayed at one of the many wayside inns built along the main routes leading to Detroit. At Wayne, Stephen G. Simmons successfully owned and operated one such inn, and the steady income from his popular establishment comfortably supported him, his invalid wife, and two adult daughters who still lived at home. Simmons, a massive, impeccably dressed man, impressed his eastern lodgers with his refined, educated speech and cultured, gentle manner.

But Simmons was also a hard drinker who, when drunk, picked fights with his friends and neighbors then beat them viciously. Simmons' own wife and daughters lived in terror because of his violent temper, and, when drunk, he had beaten the three women several times.

One late spring evening in 1830, Simmons arrived home drunk and in an ugly mood. Storming into the room where his feeble wife lay in bed, he shoved a whiskey jug next to her face and insisted that she drink with him. Hoping to appease him, his wife took several drinks, but Simmons insisted she drink more. When she refused, the 250-pound man drew back his huge fist and, as his terrified daughters tried to restrain him, he hit his wife in the head with such force that the blow killed her instantly.

Simmons was arrested, brought to Detroit, tried, and, based on the testimony of his two daughters, found guilty of murder. The court then sentenced Simmons to be hanged on September 24, 1830.

Entertainment was scarce at that time, so the Michigan Territory buzzed with excitement and controversy over the scheduled hanging. Wayne County Sheriff Thomas Knapp, a strong opponent of capital punishment, resigned rather than act as hangman, but Benjamin Woodworth, proprietor of the then-famous Steamboat Hotel, eagerly volunteered. Woodworth erected a quadrangle grandstand of plank benches for spectators and asked a local military band to provide music. The day before the scheduled execution, a steady stream of settlers from the surrounding countryside flowed down the roads leading into Detroit. Hotels rapidly filled, and many people opened their homes to the out-state visitors. By noon the next day, September 24, 1830, more than twelve hundred spectators had jammed onto the "best" seats in the bleachers, filled the jail yard, and climbed to the roofs of surrounding buildings.

At two p.m., the military band, which had played for two hours, suddenly stopped as the heavy jail door swung open and Simmons, arm in arm with Woodworth and a deputy, marched toward the scaffold. The condemned man walked up the wooden steps, gazed sadly at the silent crowd as his death warrant was read, then, with great dignity and remorse, confessed his crime and warned the audience to "beware of strong drink."

As Woodworth positioned Simmons over the trap door and adjusted the noose around his neck, Simmons, in a strong, quality baritone voice sang:

> "Show pity, Lord, O Lord, forgive,
> Let a repenting rebel live;
> Are not Thy mercies full and free?
> May not a sinner trust in Thee?
>
> "My crimes are great, but can't surpass
> The power and glory of Thy grace,
> Great God, Thy nature hath no bound,
> So let Thy pardoning love be found."

As Simmons' voice smoothly descended during the final refrain of the hymn, the executioner stepped to one side and, at the sound of the final note, released the trap. Simmons shot through the opening and died almost instantly from a broken neck.

As a result of Simmons' impressive conduct, the gruesome, circus-like atmosphere of his execution, and Sheriff Knapp's attitude, a strong aversion to capital punishment began to develop among the people of Michigan. The anti-capital punishment fires were fanned, eight years later, by the hanging of an innocent man across the river in Ontario. Finally, in the revised code of Michigan laws which became effective March 1, 1847, Michigan became the first state in the Union to limit the punishment for murder to imprisonment at hard labor for life.

BURNED AT THE STAKE

Vicksburg
June, 1832

For more than twenty minutes, the trader cried and screamed in agony.

By the late 1820s, the "golden days" of Michigan's fur trade had passed. After 150 years of unregulated and unchecked trapping, most of Michigan had been depleted of fur-bearing animals. Detroit and Mackinac remained as major clearinghouses and shipping depots, but most individual traders and trappers moved west out of Michigan.

One of the few who did stay was Conrad Wesner, and, as furs became practically extinct, the trader spent more time drinking than trading. One June afternoon in 1832, while drinking with some Potawatomi Indians at their village near (present-day) Vicksburg, Wesner saw a squaw carry a dozen mink pelts into her lodge. Wesner rushed to her lodge and tried desperately for over an hour to trade for the rare furs. When the squaw adamantly refused, Wesner flew into a drunken rage, shot and killed her, grabbed the mink pelts, and fled into the surrounding forest.

The Potawatomies quickly captured him, and, at twilight, more than a hundred painted braves, led by their chief and chanting loudly, brought the prisoner to a small hill. The chief signaled, and several Indians bound Wesner to an oak tree with deer-hide thongs. The Indians then danced in a circle around the tree while carefully piling twigs and branches around Wesner who whimpered and pleaded for his life.

The chief signaled again, and a brave lit the fire. As the flames shot upward, each Indian took turns throwing more wood onto the fire. The Indians placed the wood so that Wesner would suffer and burn slowly, and, for more than twenty minutes, he cried and screamed in agony. Finally, his screams stopped, but the Indians continued dancing and throwing wood on the fire until after midnight. Then, as the flames of the death fire died down, the Potawatomies made one last circle, waved their tomahawks and rifles triumphantly, and vanished into the darkness.

By morning, only a charred tree and warm ashes remained.

I AM HAPPY TO DIE

Sault Ste. Marie
July, 1836

They would probably say, "The savage should have been tortured first."

To most white explorers, missionaries, traders, and settlers, Indian justice, like that applied to Wesner, often seemed crude, violent, and uncivilized. But, at least in most cases, Indian justice was applied consistently and fairly, even to whites who broke Indian laws.

The "civilized" white man's law, on the other hand, often applied differently to Indians than whites. So thought Wau-bau-ne-me-kee as he stepped smiling up to the gallows.

Three weeks before, as Wau-bau-ne-me-kee and his beautiful young bride slept soundly in their Chippewa lodge near Sault Ste. Marie, five drunk white men had suddenly burst through the doorway. Two men grabbed the young brave and held him while the other three jerked his bride from the floor, tugged at her clothes, and, while laughing and taunting, tried to kiss and fondle her.

Suddenly, one of the men grunted, "Let's get serious," tore off her deerskin robe, and prepared to seriously assault her. In a furious burst of strength, Wau-bau-ne-me-kee broke free, lunged at the attacker, and, while the other four whites fled, stabbed him to death.

Wau-bau-ne-me-kee was quickly arrested, tried, and

sentenced to be hanged at Mackinac Island. As he stepped up to the gallows, the young Chippewa brave smiled and said, "I am happy to die, for I am innocent in the eyes of the Great Spirit. Any man who comes to the Indian wigwam in the dead of night and drags a wife from her husband's bosom for evil purpose is a wicked monster that should be removed from the earth.

"If an Indian were to go to a white man's house and commit the same crime and were killed, no one would say, 'Too bad.' In fact, they probably would say, 'The savage should have been tortured first,' and reward the man who killed such a wicked savage. This is what would happen if the Indian would have done what the white man did."

THEY KILT ME

Dixboro
September 27 - November 6, 1845

She leaned over and grasped her bowels in one hand and in the other held a phial containing a liquid.

Isaac VanWoert, a carpenter from Livingston County, New York, dreamed of achieving prosperity and independence in a young city founded in 1823 in the midst of lush groves of Washtenaw County, Michigan. Van-Woert had heard that his services would be in great demand in the rapidly growing area, and, in September, 1845, he, his wife, and two little boys set out by covered wagon for Ann Arbor.

As they passed through Dixboro on September 24, the VanWoerts noticed the unfinished frame of a house and asked the owner if he needed a carpenter to help him finish it. The owner not only immediately hired Van-Woert but also recommended another house that the VanWoerts could rent and live in. By that evening, the VanWoerts had settled in the house in which Martha Mulholland had suddenly died a few weeks earlier.

In a statement sworn before a justice of the peace at Ann Arbor on December 8, 1845, and printed in a number of newspapers, VanWoert told what happened next:

"On Saturday night, the 27th of September, between 7 and 8 o'clock, I was standing in front of the window of said house; my wife had stepped into Mrs. Hammond's about two rods distant, my two little boys were in the backyard, for I had just passed through the house to the front yard and was combing my hair when I saw a light through the window. I put my hand on the windowsill and looked in. I saw a woman with a candlestick in her hand in which was a candle burning. She held it in her left hand. She was a middling-sized woman; had a white cloth around her head, her right hand clasped in her clothes near the waist. She was a little bent forward, her eyes large and much sunken, very pale indeed; her lips projected, and her teeth showed some. She moved slowly across the floor until she entered the bedroom and closed the door. I then went up and opened the bedroom door, and all was dark. I stepped forward and lighted a candle with a match, looked forward but saw no one, nor heard any noise, except just before I opened the bedroom door I thought I heard one of the bureau drawers open and shut.

"I spoke of what I had seen several days after, and then learned for the first time that the house in which I then lived had been previously occupied by a widow Mulholland, and she had died there.

"The second time I saw her was in October about one o'clock in the morning. I got up, started to go out of the back door. As I opened the bedroom door it was light in the outer room. I saw no candle, but I saw the same woman that I had seen before. I was about five feet from her. She said, 'Don't touch me — touch me not.' I stepped back a little and asked her what she wanted. She said, 'He has robbed me. He got it little by little, until they kilt me! They kilt me! Now he has got it all.' I then asked her who had it all. She said, 'James, James. Yes, James has got it at last, but it won't do him long. Joseph! Oh, Joseph! I wish Joseph would come away.' Then all was dark and still.

"The third time I saw her I awoke in the night, know not the hour; the bedroom was entirely light. I saw no candle, but saw the same woman. She said, 'James can't hurt me anymore. No! He can't. I am out of his reach. Why don't they get Joseph away? Oh, my boy! Why not come away?' And all dark and still.

"The fourth time I saw her was about eleven o'clock p.m. I was sitting with my feet on the stove hearth. My family had retired and I saw the same woman in the door, supported in the arms of a man whom I knew. She was stretched back and looked as if she was in the agonies of death. She said nothing, but the man said, 'She is dying. She will die.' And all disappeared and the door closed without noise.

"The fifth time I saw her was a little after sunrise. I came out of the house to go to my work and I saw the same woman in the front yard. She said, 'I wanted Joseph to keep my papers, but they are . . .' Here something seemed to stop her utterance. Then she said, 'Joseph! Joseph! I fear something will befall my boy.' And all was gone.

"The sixth time I saw her was near midnight. It was the same woman standing in the bedroom. The room was again light as before, no candle was visible. I looked at my wife, fearing she might awake. She then raised her hand and said, 'She will not awake.' She seemed to be in great pain; she leaned over and grasped her bowels in one hand and in the other held a phial containing a liquid. I asked her what it was. 'The doctor said it was Balm of Gilead,' she replied, and all disappeared.

"The seventh time I saw her, I was working at a little bench which was standing in the room, and which I worked on in the evenings. I saw the same woman. 'I wanted to tell James something, but I could not, I could not.' I asked her what she wanted to tell. 'Oh, he did an awful thing to me.' I asked her who did. 'The man they would not let me have,' she answered. I asked her what he did. 'Oh! He gave me a great deal of trouble in my mind,' she replied. 'Oh! They kilt me! They kilt me!' she repeated several times. I walked forward and tried to reach her, but she kept the same distance from me. I asked her if she had taken anything that had killed her. She answered, 'Oh, I don't . . . Oh, I don't . . .' the froth in her mouth seemed to stop her utterance. Then she said, 'Oh, they kilt me.' I asked her, 'Who killed you?' 'I will show you,' she said. Then she went out of the back door near the fence, and I followed her. There I saw two men whom I knew, standing. They looked cast down and dejected. I saw them begin at the feet and melt down like lead melting until they were entirely melted; then a blue blaze two inches thick burned over the surface of the melted mass. Then all began bubbling up like lime slacking. I turned to see where the woman was, but she was gone. I looked back again and all was gone and dark.

"The next time I saw the woman was in the backyard, about five o'clock p.m. She said, 'I want you to tell James to repent. Oh! If he would repent. But he won't, he can't. John was a bad man,' and muttered something I could not understand. Then she said, 'Do you know where Frain's Lake is?' She then asked another question of much importance, and said, 'Don't tell of that.'

"I asked her if I should inform the public on the two men that had killed her. She replied, 'There will be a time. The time is coming. The time will come. But, oh, their end! Their end! Their wicked end!' She muttered something about Joseph, and all was dark.

"The last time I saw her was on the sixth of November, about midnight, in the bedroom. She was dressed in white; her hands hung down by her side; she stood very straight and looked very pale. She said, 'I don't want anybody here, I don't want anybody here,' and muttered over something I did not understand, except now and then the word Joseph. She then said, 'I wanted to tell a secret, and I thought I had.' And all was gone and dark.

"In all her conversation, she used the Irish accent; intermixed in all her conversation was the expression very

often repeated, 'They have kilt me, oh, they have kilt me!'
and also the name Joseph."

After hearing VanWoert's remarkable story, the justice
of the peace ordered Mary Mulholland's body exhumed,
and the coroner determined that she had been poisoned.
Authorities suspected, but could not prove, that James
Mulholland, brother of Martha's late husband John, had
swindled money and property from Martha and her 15-
year-old son Joseph. Then, with the help of a traveling
herb peddler who pretended to be a doctor, James, they
speculated, poisoned the widow.

WHO KILLED
JAMES SCHOOLCRAFT?

Sault Ste. Marie
July 6, 1846

*The white Indian swore revenge and threatened the wholesale
slaughter of all the people he thought had wronged him.*

In the summer of 1789, nine-year-old John Tanner left
the clearing in front of his Kentucky wilderness cabin to
fill his straw hat with walnuts from the surrounding

forest. Moving through the same forest were two Chippewa Indians, a father and a son, from the Saginaw Valley of Michigan. The elder warrior's squaw had so deeply mourned the accidental death of their youngest son that the two had set out on a search for a white boy to replace him. By chance, they came upon young Tanner, captured him, and carried him back to Michigan.

Tanner's Indian mother treated him kindly, but the men in his adoptive family starved, beat and overworked the young boy. Finally, disgusted by Tanner's pale face and long flowing blond hair, the boy's Chippewa father cut him down with a tomahawk blow and left him for dead. Tanner barely survived, but only to be sold, in 1792, to an Ottawa squaw from (present-day) Petoskey for ten gallons of rum. In 1800, Tanner moved with his Ottawa family to the Red River country of Manitoba, married an Indian girl, raised a family, and lived as an Indian for nearly twenty years. Tanner adapted easily to Indian life, spoke their language fluently, and excelled at hunting, fishing, and other Indian skills.

Yet Tanner despised Indians, and, in 1819, he moved his family to Mackinac. There, he spent the next nine years sporadically working as an interpreter for the government, missionaries, and fur trading companies. During that time, Tanner, who loathed Indians, also shunned whites, and his mysterious, anti-social, and often violent behavior isolated him from both worlds.

In 1828, as an act of charity, Henry Rowe Schoolcraft, scientist, author, and Indian authority, hired Tanner to serve as his interpreter at Sault Ste. Marie. But after only a few months, Schoolcraft could no longer tolerate Tanner's insane rages and fired him saying, "He is a gray-bearded, hard-featured old man whose feelings are at war with everyone on earth, white or red. He is more suspicious, revengeful, and bad-tempered than any Indian I ever knew."

Over the next eighteen years, Tanner became a total outcast. Sault Ste. Marie residents objected to his cruel treatment of his family, and, at the urging of Henry Schoolcraft, the Michigan Territorial Legislature enacted an unprecedented special law on June 10, 1830, which authorized the sheriff to take Tanner's daughter from the Sault and place her in a safe mission. Tanner later separated from his Indian wife and married a white chambermaid from Detroit. When he tried to force her to live as an Indian wife and threatened to kill her when she refused, Reverend Abel Bingham took up a collection, and the townspeople paid the woman's passage back to Detroit. Tanner swore revenge and threatened to kill H. R. Schoolcraft, Reverend Bingham, and any other townspeople he thought had wronged him over the years.

One of the few people Tanner did not threaten was James Schoolcraft, who, outside the shadow of his famous brother, Henry, had quietly established a reputation as a successful trader and chief provisioner to the garrison at Ft. Brady. But James Schoolcraft had made an enemy of his own. Lieutenant Bryant P. Tilden, while serving at Ft. Brady, had publicly threatened to kill James after fighting with him over a woman. On July 4, 1846, James Schoolcraft and Tilden, apparently setting their differences temporarily aside, celebrated the holiday in the company of other army officers. That same evening, John Tanner's house mysteriously burned to the ground, and the white Indian disappeared.

Two evenings later, James Schoolcraft walked down a path to a cleared field at the rear of his house. As

Schoolcraft passed an area of thick undergrowth, an unknown assailant shot from a distance of less than four feet. An ounce ball and three buckshot blasted into Schoolcraft's right side with such force that it blew him cleanly out of the light slippers he wore. The ounce ball pierced Schoolcraft's heart and he fell dead on his face, the empty slippers marking his final steps.

Investigators quickly concluded that the fatal shot had been fired from an army musket. But a wad of paper, also found at the murder site, had come from a hymn-book at a mission often visited by John Tanner, and the horror-stricken community concluded that the white Indian was the murderer. Troops and vigilantes, eagerly led by Lt. Tilden, scoured the countryside looking for Tanner and, according to one rumor, caught and secretly killed him. But others, for the rest of the summer, reported seeing Tanner lurking in the woods and swamps around Sault Ste. Marie.

If John Tanner lived, he never again returned to either the white or Indian world.

Shortly after the murder, Lt. Tilden and his garrison left to fight in the Mexican-American War. Tilden never returned to Michigan and died in Boston December 27, 1859.

LIFE IS CHEAP

Ontonagon
January 26, 1854

Hocking took quick and violent action against the man who had violated his property rights.

Upper Peninsula copper had beckoned to men for centuries, but few could reach it and fewer still could get it out of the ground. Ornaments, tools, and weapons hammered out of loose pieces of copper by Upper Peninsula Indians attracted the attention of French explorers who searched for, but never found, the source of the metal. In 1771, Alexander Henry, one of the few English survivors of the Ft. Michilimackinac massacre (see p. 26), organized a copper mining company but, after one bitterly cold winter of fruitless labor near the Ontonagon River, abandoned the project. Henry's reports of fabulous copper riches attracted Lewis Cass and a scientific expedition to the Ontonagon River in 1820 where they visited the site of a massive copper boulder. Twenty-one years later, state geologist Douglass Houghton confirmed the three-ton, pure copper rock's existence and also reported finding vast copper deposits throughout the Ontonagon area, Keweenaw Peninsula, and near Portage Lake. But, because of the severe climate and potentially hostile Chippewas who held title to the land, few men dared venture to the isolated region to prospect and mine.

But, in 1842, the federal government bought the entire western Upper Peninsula from the Chippewas, immediately opened it to mining, and the copper rush was on. Thousands of men armed with picks, shovels, and explosives flocked to the new frontier with one goal in mind: get rich quickly and return to wherever home was. During this quick, violent exploitation, these first miners, who arrived far ahead of the law, lived by a simple code: life is nothing, property is everything. If a man interferes with your property, kill him.

Henry Hocking lived by that code, and, when Pat Dolan violated his property rights, Hocking took quick and violent action. Hocking laid claim to property along one of the many roads that began at the Ontonagon River and threaded its way along the easiest grades of the rugged, copper-bearing hills to the inland deposits. At intervals along Hocking's road, miners, dressed in slouch hats, flannel shirts, and moccasins lived in cheap, rough cabins lit by candlelight and warmed by fires. Hocking's crude, jerry-built shanty served as a public bar for these miners, so, when Pat Dolan began building a rival bar directly across the road on land claimed by Hocking, Hocking threatened to kill him.

During the early evening, January 26, 1854, Dolan walked down the road to the river landing to pick up supplies, and, while he was gone, Hocking smashed his rival's bar into kindling wood with an axe. Dolan returned later that starlit, midwinter night and, finding his shanty in ruins, built a good-sized fire, gathered some friends, and proceeded to rebuild the structure.

Hocking, hearing the hammering and seeing the fire, pulled on his boots and strode into the firelight. "What's going on here?" he roughly asked a man who was throwing wood onto the fire. The man, spotting a pistol under Hocking's shirt, nervously stuttered something about "just putting wood on the fire" and backed nervously away.

Dolan heard the conversation and stepped out of the cabin into the light. "This is my land and I told you you couldn't build here," said Hocking as he reached under his red flannel shirt. Dolan, now surrounded by several other workers, sarcastically replied, "So, sue me."

"Damn you, I will put a ball right through you," said Hocking as he pulled his pistol and fired. Dolan screamed, "Oh, my Lord, I'm a dead man," as he fell dead into the snow.

Dolan's blood streaked the white snow as his companions dragged his body away, and Hocking, having enforced the code, walked calmly back to his bar.

ASSASSINATING THE KING

Beaver Island
June 16, 1856

As his power grew, Strang intruded more and more into the intimate daily lives of his subjects, and rumors of an assassination circulated around the island.

As the entire country's attention focused on the

thousands of Michigan residents, out-of-staters, and foreign immigrants who rushed to the Upper Peninsula copper country, another small group of newcomers arrived unnoticed on Beaver Island. In 1846, 35-year-old James Jesse Strang, leader of a band of Mormons who opposed the selection of Brigham Young as their leader, took his followers from Nauvoo, Illinois, to Voree, Wisconsin. A year later, Strang and about twenty-five loyal disciples landed on Michigan's Beaver Island.

Strang decided that the place was an ideal spot for his Mormon colony, summoned the rest of the group from Wisconsin, and, on July 8, 1850, proclaimed himself their king. Strang commanded absolute power over his followers and ruled his island kingdom with cruelty and violence. As the Mormon population approached nearly a thousand, he ordered the island's Gentile "unbelievers" out of their homes and herded them to a small colony on the island's north end. Bands of raiding Mormons stole freely from these Gentiles and any mainland fishermen who ventured too close. As a warning to all islanders and mainlanders, the raiders shot and killed an island "unbeliever," buried his body in a conspicuous place, and piled the grave high with stones.

King Strang, the only absolute monarch in America's history, did not treat his Mormon subjects much better. During the harsh winters, he left his supporters to nearly freeze or starve to death while he lived in comfort in mainland cities. Strang also set up a whipping post and flogged anyone who failed to obey his every command. His own wife and children, disgusted with his cruelty and sudden practice of polygamy, returned to Wisconsin in 1850.

Following his coronation, King Strang gained even

more power over the island's residents when he successfully ran for the state legislature, and, during his term, persuaded his colleagues to make the Beaver Islands a separate county of "Manitou" under his control. As his power grew, Strang intruded more and more into even the intimate daily lives of his subjects. In 1856, Strang ordered all the women in his kingdom to wear short dresses and a new type of underwear called "bloomers." Two women, Mrs. Thomas Bedford and Mrs. Alexander Wentworth, flatly and adamantly refused, so Strang ordered Mrs. Bedford lashed to the post and publicly whipped seventy-five times. The ladies' husbands seethed in anger, and even Strang's most ardent supporters deeply resented the intimate intrusion into their lives. Rumors of an assassination plot circulated around the island.

In mid-June, 1856, the warship *Michigan* anchored in the island's St. James Harbor, and Strang, thinking the ship had been sent to protect him, as a state legislator, from the rumored assassination, willingly accepted an invitation to come aboard. Strang stepped onto the dock leading to the ship unaware that Thomas Bedford and Alexander Wentworth waited behind some piles of cordwood. As Strang reached the end of the dock, Bedford stepped calmly behind him and, in full view of many of the *Michigan*'s crew and officers who did nothing to interfere with the attackers or warn Strang, shot the king behind the top of the left ear with a horse pistol. The bullet cracked through the top of Strang's head, and he fell to the dock. Strang looked into the eyes of the two assassins as Wentworth calmly bent down, placed a revolver to Strang's right temple, and squeezed off a shot. As Wentworth then moved to shoot Strang in the back, Bedford beat the king's head and bearded face with his pistol.

In spite of this brutal attack, Strang lived for more than three weeks before finally dying on July 9, 1856. The captain of the *Michigan* took Wentworth and Bedford aboard and brought them to Mackinac where cheering mobs of well-wishers greeted them.

HEY, COUSIN JACK

Rockland
April 24, 1857

Seeing his two countrymen running from two Cornishmen, one with a knife, James Ryan grabbed an axe and swung viciously.

At about the same time King Strang moved to Beaver Island, well-financed eastern mining companies moved into the copper country and displaced the inefficient, lone miner-prospector equipped with only hand tools. In 1847, the Minesota (sic) mine, which contained the richest, largest masses of copper ever discovered in the Upper Peninsula, opened near Rockland and employed thousands of men, the large majority of whom were Irish and Cornish immigrants.

The Cornish and Irish despised and antagonized each

other, and, beneath the copper foundation of the picturesque village of Rockland, the fuse of a destructive explosion slowly burned. The Cornish had come to Michigan copper mines in the 1850s, when copper and tin in the mines of their native English peninsula of Cornwall ran out. The mining companies usually hired the experienced and expert Cornish as shift bosses and mine captains, and the Cornish considered themselves superior to their Irish laborers. The Roman Catholic Irish immigrants, on the other hand, many of whom had fled northern Ireland during the great potato famine of 1845, spoke fervently of their hate for protestant Englishmen such as their Cornish Methodist bosses.

St. Patrick's Day of 1857 passed without violence, but, on Sunday, April 24, the burning fuse of animosity exploded into violence. Two Irishmen swaggered out of James Ryan's saloon and, spotting Richard Kissel, began taunting the Cornish shift boss. "Hey, Cousin Jack," they said, "that's a nice suit you have on. Why don't you wear it to work since you never get close enough to the ore to get it dirty."

Kissel turned and strode angrily toward the Irishmen, one of whom pulled a long knife and pointed it threateningly at the Cornishman. Solomon Curtis, another Cornishman, approached unnoticed from behind and suddenly yelled mockingly, "Don't fight, Kissel. It's not a fair fight. There's only two of them." The surprised Irishman turned toward Curtis who kicked the knife out of the attacker's hand, picked it up, and, with Kissel, chased the Irishmen back toward Ryan's saloon.

Seeing his two customers and countrymen running from two Cornishmen, one with a knife, James Ryan, owner of the saloon, grabbed an axe, charged into the street, and swung viciously at Curtis. Curtis ducked, and the axe hit Johnson Terrell in the right side just above the hip, sliced easily through the innocent bystander's ribs and bowels, and cracked to a stop against his backbone. Curtis grabbed the axe, pinned Ryan to the ground with it for a moment, then let him go so that he could help carry Terrell, who had nearly been cut in two, to a nearby house.

As Rockland's doctor followed the large red streak through the snow to the house where Terrell lay, several hundred Cornishmen gathered outside talking excitedly but in subdued tones. The doctor walked up to Terrell, took one look at the ghastly wound, felt the Cornishman's pulse, and pronounced him dead.

The Cornish mob screamed wildly, cried for revenge, and threatened to kill every Irishman in Rockland. The mob soon cornered Ryan and his Irish compatriots in Ryan's saloon. As they smashed windows, set fire to the place, and demanded that Ryan surrender, the murderer leaped from the roof and ran to an unknown fate. Many miners claimed that the Cornishmen caught Ryan, killed him with his own axe, dismembered his body, and hid it. Others said that Ryan fled into the harsh wilderness and died of exposure, and that hungry animals had devoured his body. The Irish laborers said that Ryan successfully escaped to Detroit where his wife, who collected money from the county for damages to the saloon, later joined him.

Only one fact is certain: James Ryan disappeared from Rockland forever.

THE END OF A DREAM
Flushing
February 26, 1859

For Francesca, the dream turned into a scandalous nightmare and murder.

Even in his wildest dreams, Thomas Ludwell Lee Brent probably could not have imagined himself as a pioneer settler in the rugged Saginaw Valley wilderness of Michigan. As a descendant of Britain's King Edward II and one of the founding families of the state of Virginia, Brent was accustomed to living in comfort and style. His family's wealth and influence allowed him, at age twenty-seven, to live in Spain where, in 1812, he married a sixteen-year-old Spanish countess named Francesca. Two years later, with the help of his uncle, a U.S. senator, Brent was appointed as a diplomatic secretary to Spain, then served as *charge d'affairs* to Portugal from 1825 to 1834. While living abroad, Thomas and Francesca had two children, Charlotte and Henry.

When in 1834 Portugal broke diplomatic relations with the United States, Brent and his family returned to his lavish Virginia estate. But Brent's neighbors disapproved of his beautiful Spanish wife and blackballed the couple from society. When in defiance Brent threatened to relocate his entire estate and wealth, a Washington friend, Lewis Cass, suggested that he move to the unexplored Saginaw Valley of Michigan.

Cass himself had, in 1819, negotiated a treaty with the

Indians that opened most of Michigan to white settlement. But, under the conditions of that treaty, the Saginaw Bay Chippewas, a tribe with a well-earned reputation for hatred of whites (see p. 42) had retained hunting and fishing rights throughout the Saginaw Valley, and few whites dared disturb their hunting preserve. By 1834, whites had created and organized counties almost totally surrounding the Chippewas, but the only evidence of civilization in the Indians' valley reservation were a few settlements along a wilderness trail that stretched from Detroit to Saginaw.

In the early spring of 1836, Thomas L.L. Brent rode up this trail on horseback, bought a canoe at the tiny new settlement of Flint, paddled down the river, and examined the land near (present-day) Flushing. Brent liked what he saw and, by the time winter set in, purchased 70,000 acres of the timbered land at a cost of $1.25 an acre. Brent brought his family — Francesca, 40, Charlotte, 13, and Henry, 11 — to Genesee County and the former aristocrats settled into a log cabin just like any other pioneer family.

But Brent did not plan to stay in his log cabin long, for he had a dream — he planned to log off the land, sell parcels to other settlers and use that money to duplicate his Virginia mansion on six hundred prime acres he had reserved for himself. Brent named his Michigan estate "Barcelonia" and dreamed of bringing his horses, slaves, and carriages from Virginia and filling a fantastic house with silver plates, vintage wines, and exquisite furniture.

Though fifty-two years old, Brent pursued his dream vigorously. By the time Michigan gained statehood in 1837, he had built a small two-story frame house as a slight improvement over the log cabin and had cleared roads into the area. Brent then cleared large sections of lands for farms and constructed a small sawmill.

But Brent's dream was rudely interrupted by fiscal reality, then death. Very few settlers responded to his ads in eastern newspapers, and, because he had spent his entire fortune on the land purchase and improvements, Brent could not afford to pay the taxes on his 70,000 acres. In 1838, Brent sold a third of his land for taxes and struggled for the next seven years just to break even. On August 18, 1845, at the age of 60, Thomas L.L. Brent died of "bilious fever," and his body, which had once stood erect before royalty, had to be unceremoniously lowered out the second-story window of his house because the stairway was too narrow and crooked.

After Brent's death, Francesca, with the managerial help of the family minister, struggled to resurrect Barcelonia. She sold more pieces of land and, with the proceeds, built a lavish two-story plantation house complete with a music room. Charlotte played the piano; effeminate and frivolous Henry constructed Aeolian harps; and they enjoyed their roles as hosts at musicales at a time when few other residents had musical instruments. When tenant farmers finally began to move in and work the cleared land, the family became debt-free and the minister turned the management of the property over to Francesca.

But, for Francesca, the dream soon turned into a scandalous nightmare and murder. To Francesca's shock and shame, Charlotte carried on an affair with a tenant farmer named Palmer. When Charlotte became pregnant, Palmer's wife suddenly and mysteriously died, and he married Charlotte. On February 26, shortly after Charlotte's baby was born, Francesca died from what a jury of inquest determined was "arsenic administered by some person or persons unknown." Palmer disappeared, and Charlotte and Henry were arrested and charged with the murder of their mother. But when they were released for lack of evidence, they too disappeared, and no one from the Brent family ever set foot on Barcelonia again.

THE SHOT HEARD AROUND THE LEGAL WORLD
Seul Choix Point
June 18, 1859

Trembling with fear, Gust Pond reluctantly raised his shotgun, jerked the trigger, and changed America's legal concept of self-defense.

Augustus Pond came to Seul Choix Point from Mackinac Island to fish commercially during the summer of 1859. The Pond family lived in their "summer home," a sixteen- by sixteen-foot frame shanty with one window and one door hinged with leather straps and fastened on the inside with rope attached to a nail. Scores of other Mackinac Islanders, like Isaac Blanchard, David Plant, and Joseph Robillard, also trekked the seventy-five miles to Seul Choix, and their flimsy dwellings, net houses, and other outbuildings stretched along the isolated finger of land jutting into the northern-most reaches of Lake Michigan near Manistique.

Blanchard, Plant, and Robillard didn't like mild-mannered, inoffensive Gust Pond and bullied, harassed, and tormented him at every opportunity. On Monday, June 13, 1859, Plant, for no apparent reason, walked up to Pond, accused him of "abusing an Irishman," hit him in the face, and knocked him to the ground. The following Thursday night, Blanchard, an enormously strong and intimidating man, beat loudly on Pond's door and tugged at the thin leather hinges and rope latch while Plant and Robillard loudly threatened Pond, his wife, and three small children.

On Friday night, the three tormentors walked up to Pond's flimsy net house — six posts set in the ground, sided with boards, and roofed with bark shingles. Blanchard tore the only door from its leather hinges, shook a hired man who slept on a bunk inside, and demanded to know where Pond was. The hired man, unaware that, because of the previous night's threats, Pond had taken his family to his brother-in-law's house, said he didn't know, and Plant, Robillard, and Blanchard left.

During the cool hours just before dawn, they returned. Plant dragged the hired man from the bunk and began to choke him while Blanchard and Robillard began tearing the roof from the net house.

Hearing the hired man's cries for help and the sounds of ripping and crashing boards, Pond picked up a double-barreled shotgun he had borrowed from his brother-in-law and stepped into the moonlight. "Who's tearing down my net house," he demanded. Only the sound of shingles crashing on the ground answered him. "Leave or I'll shoot," shouted Pond. Still no answer. "Leave or I'll shoot," he repeated. Again, the sound of another section of roof ripping from its anchorage was the only reply. Pond put the gun to his shoulder and jerked the trigger, and the gun spat fire as it sent one barrel of "pigeon shot" into Blanchard's body. Plant and Robillard ran, and Blanchard staggered bleeding about seventy yards before falling dead in some bushes. Gust Pond walked to the home of his brother Louis, a constable, and surrendered.

Pond was convicted of manslaughter, but his defense lawyers argued, in an appeal before the State Supreme Court, that the killing was justifiable. Legally, self-defense had always been justification for homicide, they argued. If a person is directly attacked, that person has the right to defend himself using any means necessary, including murder. But Blanchard had not directly attacked Pond, just Pond's property, the night he was killed, so, for the first time in any court of law, Pond's lawyers took self-defense one step further arguing that "the attack on his property was so close to his dwelling that it brought grave danger to his very doorstep."

The State Supreme Court agreed and, in a landmark decision, stated that "a man assaulted in his dwelling is not obliged to retreat, but may use such means as are absolutely necessary to repel the assailant from his house . . . if the assault or breaking is felonious, the homicide becomes, at common law, justifiable . . ." The court then ordered a new trial, but Pond died before his case came to court again.

Sixty-five years later, the legal opinion resulting from Pond's moonlight blast would help Clarence Darrow save several Detroit black men from murder convictions (see p. 139).

FLAMES OF HATE

Detroit
March 6, 1863

As the heat grew more intense, one by one the men inside tried to escape.

When, in February, 1861, southern states seceded from the Union and formed the Confederate States of America, Michigan reacted quickly. On March 15, 1861, the state legislature gave the governor broad powers to furnish Michigan men to serve in a federal army to put down any rebellion against the federal government. By May 1, the state mustered the first Michigan infantry into the United States Army, and, in all, Michigan raised thirty regiments of infantry, eleven of cavalry, one of artillery, and one of sharpshooters during the Civil War.

Not all of Michigan's contributions to the Union cause were positive, however. In Detroit, on February 26, 1863, a dark-skinned man named Thomas Faulkner was arrested for allegedly molesting and raping two teenaged girls, one white and one black. Heated and hysterical tales of savage sexual outrages commited by a Negro against an innocent white girl spread rapidly through Detroit's poor immigrant white communities.

On March 3, 1863, two days before Faulkner's scheduled trial, the U.S. Congress passed a national conscription law, and federal troops arrived in Detroit to enforce the draft order. Because the law allowed the affluent to escape the draft by paying a $300 fee, Detroit's poor, unskilled German and Irish immigrants, who had vehemently objected to President Abraham Lincoln's Emancipation Proclamation, felt that they were now going to be used as cannon fodder so that black men could take their jobs.

The incensed whites, who blamed blacks for the entire war, focused their hate and rage on Thomas Faulkner. Faulkner's trial began on March 5, and, at the conclusion of the day's proceedings, while officers escorted him from the court back to jail, an angry mob surrounded the frightened prisoner and his guards. A man knocked Faulkner down with a paving stone, but the guards rushed the accused rapist to jail without further incident. The next day, Faulkner was found guilty, sentenced to life imprisonment, and the trial ended. As seventy-five federal troopers took Faulkner from the court to the jail, a mob carrying guns, clubs, axes, and a rope attacked the military guard in an attempt to lynch the convicted rapist. A few of the guards fired into the crowd, killing one man and wounding several others.

A man screamed, "If we are got to be killed up for niggers, then we will kill every nigger in town," and the mob turned and surged toward nearby black-owned businesses and homes. Robert Bennett, Joshua Boyd, Lewis Houston, and Marcus Dale, unaware of the approaching mob, were working in their employer's woodworking shop down the street from the jail when, suddenly, a paving stone smashed through the window. The four black men rushed to the window to see a mob of several hundred angry white men charging their building while screaming, "Kill all the damned niggers." As several whites tried to break down the door and bricks and stones smashed more windows, Boyd grabbed an old shotgun and fired a blast over the mob's head.

The mob backed off for a few seconds, then rushed an attached house where the black men's terrified wives and children huddled inside. When Bennett, Boyd, Houston, and Dale ran into the house to protect their families, several whites entered the abandoned shop and set it on fire. Piles of wood shavings fueled a roaring fire, and the flames quickly reached the attached house. The mob, which completely surrounded the house, allowed the screaming women and children to escape but forced the men to stay inside the burning buildings.

As the heat grew more intense, one by one the men inside tried to escape. Bennett charged out the front door and rushed through the crowd which clubbed, stoned, and shot at the fleeing man. Though knocked down five times, Bennett reached a nearby hotel whose white owner hid the bleeding man. Houston escaped through a back alley behind a fence, but members of the mob caught him when he entered the street. A vicious blow from one man's club fractured Houston's skull, and another white kicked out the black man's teeth before two sympathetic whites grabbed him and rushed him to the protection of the jail.

Marcus Dale escaped next and later described his ordeal: "I was knocked down by a stone in the yard while the house was burning, and when I came to myself enough to know anything, I found the flames so intense that I would soon be burned to death, unless I had some shelter; so I drew a wheelbarrow over me, that fortunately was just there. I was unable to walk, and there I lay till a couple of policemen came to me and dragged me out, and took me outside of the lot, and turned me loose.

"I then staggered over to Mrs. Jones', being weak from the blows and loss of blood. I had not been there but a few moments before they came and said to me: 'Get out of there.' It was, as I suppose, the same two men who took me out from under the wheelbarrow.

"I found it impossible to get away; so I got out into the privy to conceal myself, and soon a couple of fellows— one a man in soldier's clothes, and the other a man who sold in the market, named Dollar — came to me and brought me out on St. Antoine Street, beating me all the way along, the mob behind me throwing at me, and some pelting me with stones and sticks till they got me to Croghan Street; and there they fell on me, and with kicks and clubs, beat me till they thought life was extinct, and then went off and left me for dead!

"My head was bruised so that for weeks my head and ears run with corruption. My knee cap was broken right in two by a stroke from some weapon. My body was so bruised that for two days I vomited nothing but pure blood; but, through the mercy of the Lord, I am now getting better, but never shall overcome the effects of the injuries I have received."

The last man in the house, Joshua Boyd, ran into the backyard and, overcome with smoke and face badly burned, fell to his knees. Twenty rioters rushed at him and, while yelling, "Kill the nigger," clubbed the helpless former slave to death.

The howling mob then moved through the neighborhood, savagely beating black men, women, and children and ransacking stores and homes before setting them on fire. When firemen arrived, the mob slashed their hoses. Detroit, at that time, had not yet established a police department, and the U.S. Provost Marshall feared that, if he sent his troops to quell the riot, the mob would use the opportunity to free the reluctant draftees he had under guard.

So, for the next several hours, whites continued to beat and burn while hundreds of blacks fled to safety in Canada and surrounding communities. Finally, troops from nearby Fort Wayne and Ypsilanti arrived and dispersed the mob. As evening settled, flames from thirty-five burning buildings lighted the sky, and smoke drifted through the deserted streets of Detroit's black community.

Ironically, Thomas Faulkner, the dark-skinned man whose crime sparked the riot, wasn't even black but was Spanish-Indian. And, the crime itself never took place. The girls who had accused Faulkner were prostitutes who, several years later, admitted they had fabricated the story of Faulkner's rape.

FATAL OBSESSION

Woodstock Township
January, 1865

David turned toward Laura, who begged him to spare her life for the sake of her unborn child.

More than half of Michigan's military age population, over 90,000 men, served in the Union armed forces during the Civil War, and nearly 15,000 of them died. Following President Lincoln's call for men "to put down the insurrection," Michigan men rushed to join the Union Army, and, in a wave of patriotic fervor, independent companies of volunteers were raised in towns and villages across the state. When news of Lincoln's call for troops reached farmers in Mecosta County, they stopped their threshers and headed for Big Rapids where a regiment was being formed. In Calhoun County, a 36-year-old shoe store salesman organized and drilled a company of volunteers, and a Lawton man, in a slight excess of patriotism, enlisted in two different Michigan regiments. David Bivins, only son of a Woodstock Township (Lenawee County) farmer, also eventually joined the Union Army, but for a very unusual reason.

While the war raged, David's father, like most Michigan farmers, achieved a prosperity of which he never dreamed. To feed the military, the government paid David's father and other farmers record prices for their bumper crops of wheat, corn, oats, and rye. David had planned, someday, to take control of the family lands, but, as the farm flourished, he grew anxious and impatient. After marrying his second wife Laura in 1863, David's impatience turned to obsession, and he spent all his waking hours thinking up ways to obtain the thriving farm.

Finally, David came up with what he thought to be a brilliant plan. He would threaten to enlist in the army, and his parents, rather than see their only child go off to war, would deed him their home and farm. But, to David's shock, his mother and father were thrilled and proud that their son, who up until then had lacked ambition and motivation, would bring honor to their family name. To David's great disappointment, his commission came through and he received his orders.

About two weeks later, David deserted and, fearing that authorities would be watching his father's farm, met his family at his father-in-law's house. There, David's father begged him to return to his unit and regain his honor. David refused and bluntly asked his father to give him the farm. The elder Bivins stared silently at the floor for a moment, reached into his pocket for some money, and looked sadly into his son's eyes as he said, "David, it is not safe to stay here. Here is $100, the last money I will ever give you. Be gone and do not show your face in my home until you become an honest and industrious man."

David fled to Grafton, Ohio, earned a living as a Blackman's Medicine salesman, and, though still married to Laura, fell in love with a local woman named Myra Hart. David dreamed of having both Myra and his father's farm and soon hatched a sinister plot to rid himself of his pregnant wife Laura and his parents.

In January, 1865, three months before the war's end, David appeared unannounced at his father's house and, during a long, falsely sincere conversation, humbly told his family that he had reformed, wanted to earn an honorable living, and wished to return home. The elder Bivins, skeptical but hopeful, told David to go to Grafton, pick up his belongings, and return home. David went to nearby Hudson and purchased a ticket for the afternoon train east. Then, under an assumed name, he ordered a livery stable to have a light buggy and horse ready upon the arrival of the return train.

David then rode the afternoon train out of Hudson, boarded the return train under his alias, and took the rented horse and buggy to his father's house. The light buggy and horse made no sound and left no tracks on the bare frozen ground as David hid the animal and rig out of sight in some bushes. David walked into the house and told his surprised parents and wife that he had something very important to tell all of them. As they all went to the kitchen table, David seated himself next to his father, put his left arm around his father's shoulder, and pulled him near as if to say something very personal and private. Suddenly, with his right hand, David pulled a pistol from his coat pocket and shot his father through the head. As his father fell dead to the floor, Bivins turned and shot his shocked mother through the chest, killing her instantly.

David then turned toward Laura, who begged him to spare her life for the sake of their unborn child. Without speaking, David put a bullet into Laura's abdomen, killing the unborn child, and, as Laura grabbed her stomach in shock and pain, coolly shot her through the forehead. David then set fire to the house, returned to town, and took the morning train east out of Hudson.

David's coat, however, had blown out of the buggy as he raced back to town from the burning farm, and, as a result of that evidence, he was tried and convicted of the murders. Bivins spent the first five years of his prison term in solitary confinement and later died in the Michigan State Prison.

THE ONLY WAY OUT
Rogers City
August 23, 1875

Women knew that if they resisted his advances, Molitor would isolate their families without food, money, work, or way out.

Civil War veterans returned to Michigan to find a new major industry dominating their state's commercial development — the sawing, harvesting, and milling of timber. This enterprise employed tens of thousands of men, and sawmills sprang up in nearly every southern Lower Peninsula town located on the mouth of a river. Initially, logs were cut within a few miles of these mills, but, as nearby forests were quickly destroyed, speculators and entrepreneurs purchased and developed more distant stands of timber.

In 1866, while mapping the verdant wilderness area of

Presque Isle County for the federal Department of Lake Survey, William Rogers and Albert Molitor discovered a huge, valuable stand of timber which they purchased. The two decided to develop the areas themselves and, during the spring of 1869, formed the Molitor-Rogers Company which sent seventy-five German and Polish immigrants to (present-day) Rogers City. There, the company built a sawmill, a store, a boardinghouse, and a blacksmith shop, and the immigrants began harvesting the great stand of timber.

But during the extremely snowy and bitter cold winter of 1870-71, the settlers nearly starved to death, and a discouraged William Rogers gave up and turned the entire venture over to Albert Molitor. Molitor, the illegitimate son of King William I of Wurtemburg, eagerly took full and direct control of the village and lured newcomers to the area with glowing ads in Detroit and Cleveland ethnic newspapers.

As the town rapidly grew, the handsome, overbearing, and cruel Molitor became a virtual dictator of the isolated community. Molitor's well-stocked store, the only one in town, charged exorbitant prices for food and clothing. As the town's sole employer, Molitor demanded fourteen-hour days at the mill or in the woods. And, if another man's wife or daughter appealed to him, he would walk into her house and make love to her. The women knew that if they resisted his advances, Molitor would fire their husbands or fathers and isolate them without food, money, work, or way out. A several hundred mile walk down the coast or through the surrounding uncharted forest offered the only escape route. A steamer, arriving weekly from Detroit during the navigation season, provided the only limited contact with the outside world.

The immigrants, who had come to this country to escape just such treatment, hated Molitor and, by 1875 organized against the dictator. On August 20, 1875, Andrew E. Banks, a well-educated German lawyer and preacher, called a meeting of the twelve men he knew most hated Molitor, swore them to secrecy, and unveiled an assassination plot. Three days later, while Banks visited a neighbor to establish an alibi, a vigilante group rode into town, surrounded Molitor's store, and fired a fusillade of shots through his office window. The bullets killed a young clerk instantly, but Molitor, though severely wounded, was able to board the weekly steamer to Detroit where he died on September 18, 1875.

Most of the townspeople rejoiced at Molitor's murder, and, though stories were whispered behind closed doors, no one, for fifteen years, discussed the murder publicly, and no one was charged with the crime. Finally, in 1891, one of the town's earliest settlers, William Repke, overcome with guilt, confessed to the murder of Albert Molitor and named ten accomplices. In 1893, Repke and four others were convicted and sentenced to life imprisonment. Four years later, Governor Hazen Pingree pardoned all but Repke.

BLINKY'S HAMMER
Bay City
Late Summer, 1875

Fournier got drunk, butted and tore apart a bandstand, and fought with Blinky Robertson, another Bay City tough.

From September to March, lumberjacks spent six days a week, sunup to sundown, at rigorous, dangerous, and tedious work. They lived in depressing, windowless bunkhouses; alcohol was banned so, for relaxation, the lumberjacks chewed tobacco and fought. Every camp and sawmill town claimed its own "tough guy," the best, meanest figher, and when two of the best met, entire towns poured onto the streets and on top of rooftops and railroad boxcars to witness the great event.

Two of the best fighting men in Michigan lumberjack history, "Silver Jack" Driscoll and Joe "Frenchy" Fournier, met, in 1870, at the Red Keg Saloon in Averill, and their battle turned into legend. Fournier opened the bout by lunging at Silver Jack and grabbing his throat with both hands. Both giants crashed to the floor, and Fournier squeezed so hard that Driscoll's eyes bulged and rolled unnaturally. For an hour, all Silver Jack could do was occasionally loosen Fournier's death grip and catch a breath. Fournier responded by squeezing even harder and butting Jack in the face with his rock-hard head.

When Jack's tongue began to roll out of his mouth, Fournier, in order to get more leverage to finish Driscoll, put one foot on a brass rail attached to the front of the bar. With a last desperate kick, Silver Jack drove the heel of his lumberjack boot, with its long pointed steel calks, into Fournier's foot. Fournier bellowed, let go of Jack's throat, and both men leaped to their feet.

Fournier then tried to butt Driscoll, lowering his head and, like a billy goat, running at Jack. But at each rush, like a bullfighter, Jack would step aside at the last second, and Fournier would crash into the bar, often splitting the heavy oak. Fournier made a final charge, and Jack, instead of stepping aside, drove a solid blow into the pit of Fournier's stomach, ending the match immediately.

Silver Jack went on to spend fourteen years in Jackson prison for two separate convictions for armed robbery before dying in bed at a L'Anse boardinghouse in 1895.

Joe Fournier stayed in the area and, on a late summer day in 1875, joined a Bay City group for a picnic at Bay View at the mouth of the Kawkawlin River. Fournier got drunk, butted and tore apart a bandstand at the park, and fought with several men, including Adolphous "Blinky" Robertson, another Bay City tough. When the steamer returned to Bay City just after dark, Fournier staggered down the gangplank at the Third Street dock. Following close behind was Blinky Robertson who suddenly swung a large steel ship's carpenter's mallet hitting Fournier over the head so hard that, according to one witness, "It drove his feet six inches into the hard-packed sawdust."

Blinky was tried for murder and found not guilty. Fournier's massive, thick-boned skull with rows of double teeth was used as evidence at the trial and was displayed for years after at the Bay City courthouse.

FOR GOD'S SAKE, BOYS, DON'T LEAVE ME

Dexter
January 20, 1878

Morand exploded out of his hut, axe in hand, and swung a blow at Cavanaugh.

In November, 1877, W.H. Morand, a middle-aged bearded, black man, leased a small piece of land along the Michigan Central railroad tracks near Dexter and built a crude hut of saplings bent down and covered with earth and brush. There, the recluse, who believed himself to be the "savior," often entertained Thomas O'Grady, Steve Cavanaugh, and several other young Dexter men with vivid descriptions and wild details arising from his belief that he possessed unlimited knowledge of the past, present, and future.

After several visits, the young men concluded that Morand was a bit daft but harmless and decided to have a bit of fun of their own. On Sunday morning, January 20, 1878, O'Grady, Cavanaugh, and six other young men arrived at Morand's hut and agitated the "savior" by pelting him with rocks and sticks. As Morand retreated to his crude dwelling he told the men to stop, but they continued, and, when Morand disappeared inside, Cavanaugh placed a large log across his doorway.

Suddenly, Morand exploded out of his hut, axe in hand, and swung a blow at Cavanaugh. As Cavanaugh jumped out of the way, O'Grady pulled a revolver and fired in the air close to Morand's head hoping to scare him. This enraged Morand even more, and he cracked the axe into O'Grady's shoulder, knocking him to the ground. The other seven men, overcome with horror by the sight of O'Grady's gushing blood, ran in all directions as O'Grady screamed, "For God's sake, boys, don't leave me." Then, as the stunned O'Grady slowly rose to his knees in a stooping position, Morand raised the axe executioner style and split the young man's head. He then mashed and mutilated O'Grady's skull with two more blows before carrying the body fifteen feet and throwing it into a ditch on the other side of the track.

Morand then walked to the village of Dexter and surrendered. He was tried, judged insane, and sent to the Kalamazoo State Hospital for the Insane.

SLAUGHTER OF THE PASSENGER PIGEON

Petoskey
March - June, 1878

The passenger pigeon once flew in Michigan skies in flocks so large they blocked out the sun for hours.

At the same time lumbermen were destroying Michigan's vast white pine forests, hunters and fishermen wantonly slaughtered much of the state's wildlife. In 1880, commercial hunters shipped the meat of more than 100,000 Michigan deer to national markets. Some fishermen used dynamite in inland lakes, and, in 1871, one party fishing along the AuSable River caught so many grayling that they left more than two thousand on the shore to rot. Bird hunters, many using a punt gun, a small cannon on a pole that fired a half pound of ball shot at a time, killed so many quail, grouse, and prairie chickens that, by 1865, those birds had completely disappeared in many southern Michigan areas.

The passenger pigeon, too, once flew in Michigan skies in flocks so large they blocked out the sun for hours. The beautiful birds arrived in Michigan in March and remained until early autumn. During that time, professional hunters systematically attacked the pigeons' nesting places, killed the birds, salted them, and sold them for $2 apiece to Chicago and New York restaurant buyers. In 1874, at one nesting colony in Michigan, professional hunters killed 25,000 pigeons a day for twenty-eight straight days.

But the most devastating murder of the birds occurred in Petoskey from March through June, 1878. During that time, professional hunters, using poles, guns, axes, nets, and fires, slaughtered more than one million passenger pigeons. The systematic massacres continued until the last wild passenger pigeon, it is believed, was shot in Pike County, Ohio, on March 24, 1900. Martha, the last bird of the passenger pigeon species, died at the Cincinnati Zoo on September 1, 1914.

HEY, RUBE!

Chesaning
June 6, 1881

The performance abruptly stopped, and performers and helpers grabbed tent stakes and raced for the opening.

Chesaning's children buzzed with excitement when, in May, 1881, a man tacked up large posters that announced the rare coming, in June, of the "great Hilliard and DeMott Circus and menagerie of wild animals." The circus would be a pleasurable change from the village's normal summer entertainment — brawling and drunk lumberjacks who came to town from Saginaw Valley camps at the close of the lumbering season and staged informal races and feats of strength.

Chesaning's adults, too, prepared for the arrival of the circus and the crowds it would attract. To handle the expected overflow of people who would flood into the village from the surrounding countryside and other small towns in the area, the owners of Chesaning's largest bar and hotel built a "bowery," an outdoor drinking and dancing pavilion, very near to where the circus tent would be erected. And the village council, anticipating trouble from the rumored "rowdy" circus employees, swore in ten extra untrained police officers.

Word of the council's mistrust reached the traveling circus while en route to Chesaning, and they arrived irritable, sullen, and resentful. And when the circus owners spotted the bowery, which they felt would cut deeply into their show's attendance and profits, they became enraged.

Several of the showmen met and devised a plan to both destroy the bowery and embarrass the amateur, temporary police officers — two of their men would deliberately provoke a fight at the bowery then, when attacked, would signal those in the circus tent for help and, in the ensuing excitement, would tear down the flimsy bowery. On the night of June 6, 1881, several hundred men, women, and children watched the circus evening performance while others drank, danced, and partied a few hundred yards away at the bowery. At ten p.m., just before the final act of the show, two tough, dirty circus employees left the tent, entered the crowded bowery, and, pretending they were drunk, insulted several women and bumped, cursed, and pushed the men. A fight broke out between one of the partyers and circus men. As Gus Emery, a volunteer deputy, tried to break up the scuffle, the other troublemaker ran back to the circus tent, burst through the closed flaps, and yelled, "Hey, Rube!" At this prearranged signal, the performance abruptly stopped, and fifteen performers and helpers grabbed tent stakes and raced for the opening. Screaming, "Let's clean out this whole stinking town," they charged the bowery.

But instead of destroying the property as planned, the mob fiercely and indiscriminately beat the surprised partyers and deputies. The first showmen rushed through the bowery entrance and clubbed Gus Emery on the head. As the special deputy staggered, a stocky, powerfully built, black lion trainer ran up to him and, with a covered lead ball on the end of his whip handle, shattered several of Emery's teeth then killed him with a sickening crack to the temple. Wildly swinging their clubs, the rest of the attackers quickly moved through the crowd. Women screamed, and pistol shots cracked through the night air as the seventy-five frightened drinkers, dancers, and deputies scrambled out of the bowery.

The circus mob clubbed and beat fifteen to twenty citizens as they chased the crowd from the bowery two blocks to the already packed hotel and bar. Off and on for the rest of the night, the mob threw rocks through the hotel windows where, inside, frightened men, women, and children huddled. At daylight, the frightened residents meekly emerged from the hotel to find that the circus had quietly packed up and left town.

Thirteen of the attackers were arrested at the circus' next stop, Owosso, and brought to trial in Chesaning. The lion tamer was convicted of the killing of Gus Emery, and eight others were sentenced to prison for their part in the riot and assault.

THE BLOODIED STREETS
OF MENOMINEE

Menominee
September 26, 1881

As Norman fell to the blood-spattered ground, he pulled a revolver from his shirt and emptied the cylinder.

By 1880, lumberjacks had cut more than four billion board feet of white pine from the Saginaw Valley, and, as the area rapidly turned into a depleted wilderness of stumps and slashings, lumbering operations moved to the northern Lower Peninsula and portions of the Upper Peninsula.

Brothers John and Frank McDonald left a long and embittered list of enemies when they followed the move northward to Menominee. Even their fellow "Valley Boys" (as Saginaw Valley lumberjacks were called) considered them cruel, vicious, and unfair fighters, a reputation difficult to earn among the brawling timbermen who gouged eyes, chewed off ears, and often ended a fight by jumping up and down on a beaten opponent with spike boots. But the McDonalds violated the lumberjack code of honor by stealing from their fellow workers, ganging up two-on-one against most opponents, and routinely slashing their enemies with knives.

The McDonalds continued their fighting, bullying, and lawbreaking in Menominee, and, during the winter of 1880, the Menominee County sheriff rode to their camp to make what he thought would be a routine arrest of the two huge men for a minor violation. But before the lawman reached the camp, the McDonalds jumped him and beat him unconscious. After returning to town, the battered sheriff deputized George Kittson, one of the toughest, strongest lumberjacks in the county, and sent him after the McDonalds. Kittson waited until the brothers separated, then beat each one before dragging them both to jail. The local judge found the McDonalds guilty of resisting arrest, assaulting the sheriff, and various other charges and sentenced them to a year and a half at Jackson prison.

While in prison, Frank and John McDonald became obsessed with the thought of getting even with George Kittson and, immediately upon their release, returned to Menominee. On September 26, 1881, the McDonalds swaggered boldly through the doors of saloon after Menominee saloon futilely looking for George. After an hour of searching, threatening, and drinking, they finally spotted George's half-brother Billy at the bar of the Three Chimney House Saloon. The McDonalds roughly pushed Billy back and forth between them as they demanded to know George's whereabouts. Suddenly, Billy grabbed a whiskey bottle in each hand, crashed them over the McDonalds' heads, and, as they fell stunned to the floor, ran out the back door of the saloon.

When the angry brothers regained their feet, they searched the town for Billy and found him at another bar with another Kittson brother, Norman. John McDonald invited Billy out into the street to finish what he called an unfair fight, and Billy accepted. As they walked into the sawdust-covered street, John McDonald grabbed a heavy canthook from a nearby wagon and swung it viciously at Billy's head. The weapon glanced off Billy's shoulder as he charged into the bigger McDonald and knocked him to the ground.

Suddenly, McDonald pulled a knife and plunged it between Billy's shoulder blades. Instantly, Norman leaped from the wooden sidewalk to help his wounded brother, and McDonald stabbed him in the neck and head. As Norman fell to the blood-spattered ground, he pulled a revolver from his shirt and, though he emptied the cylinder, only grazed Frank McDonald's leg. As the McDonalds jumped into a stolen horse and buggy and fled, Billy Kittson crawled onto the wooden sidewalk, struggled slowly to his feet, staggered inside to the oak bar, and fell over dead.

The sheriff quickly overtook the McDonalds a few miles outside of town, arrested them at gunpoint, and brought them to jail on a charge of first-degree murder.

The next day, an angry group of about twenty men spent the afternoon at the town's largest saloon drinking and angrily discussing the murder. By ten that evening, the drunken mob stormed the jail, broke the door down with a telephone pole, put ropes around the terrified McDonalds' necks, and jerked them into the street.

There, the lynchers tied the ropes to the back of a horse and wagon and dragged the McDonalds through the streets lined with hundreds of people who kicked the screaming men and spit on them as they bounced and tumbled by. When the mob reached the railroad tracks outside of town, they tied the two battered, bloody, and lifeless bodies to the crossing sign and threw rocks and garbage at them. The gang then hauled the bodies back to town, threw them in the street in front of the Three Chimney House and burned the building to the ground.

Two leaders of the lynch mob were arrested, and the

governor promised a thorough investigation, but within a short time, the entire matter was dropped and no one convicted of the crime.

The McDonalds went to their graves as the only lumberjacks hanged by their own breed in Michigan logging history.

DON'T KICK SO

Meredith
June 15, 1884

Few girls escaped and many disappeared.

In 1881, after spending three miserable years as a lumberjack, 26-year-old Jim Carr built a two-story, combination bar, dance hall, and whorehouse on a hill overlooking Harrison. Carr's spacious establishment, known as the "Devil's Ranch Stockade," could hold as many as three hundred of the area's lumberjacks at one time as they crowded up to the long oak bar and tossed money into large pails for booze and bad women. Business boomed, and, in 1884, Carr opened a "branch" bordello at nearby Meredith.

To provide girls for his "stockades," Carr advertised in metropolitan newspapers for hotel "waitressess" and "chambermaids." From around the state, young women arrived in Harrison, by train, expecting respectable jobs but, instead, were forced into an often short life of prostitution. Those who refused or tried to escape were beaten, often by Jim Carr himself who sometimes used brass knuckles.

Few girls escaped and many disappeared. Lumberjacks, too, "disappeared" while visiting the hotel, and Harrison's residents began referring to the site as "Dead Man's Hill" in memory of the many victims. Although implicated in many of the mysterious disappearances, Jim Carr managed to escape prosecution for more than four years.

But when Frankie Osborne, one of Carr's Meredith "waitresses," didn't disappear, Carr finally saw the inside of a jail. On the night of June 15, 1884, Carr made one of his twice-weekly visits to the Meredith ranch and, in front of the bartender and two frightened prostitutes, removed his coat, rolled up his sleeves, and began to beat Frankie. The first blow from Carr's huge fist knocked the young prostitute sprawling to the plank floor. Carr picked up the stunned girl, ordered her to square dance, and, when she shook her head "no," pounded her until she fell unconscious to the blood-spattered floor. As Carr then mercilessly kicked Frankie, she awoke for a brief moment, whispered, "Please don't kick so," and fell back unconscious. Carr, six feet tall and powerfully built, continued to beat and kick Frankie until he became exhausted. As Carr then put on his coat and left the room, he breathlessly ordered the bartender, Tom Murphy, to "finish Frankie."

Unknown to Carr, Frankie was Murphy's girlfriend, and the bartender, instead of arranging Frankie's disappearance, sent for a doctor. Frankie softly cried and whispered weakly, "Am I going to die from this?" as the doctor examined her bruised and bloody body. The doctor sadly told her that she was hemorrhaging internally and would probably die before morning, but Frankie lived for two more days.

The doctor notified authorities, who immediately took the two witnessing prostitutes into protective custody. Based on their wide-ranging testimony, a grand jury not only indicted Carr for the murder of Frankie Osborne but also for the murder of Charles Cobden, a lumberjack who had disappeared near Dead Man's Hill the previous July.

Upon hearing this surprising indictment, Carr immediately sent one of his henchmen to dig up the body of the lumberjack whom he had shot, stuffed into a large whiskey barrel, and buried under a horse carcass near his Harrison brothel. Carr's hired man dug up Cobden's body and burned it piece by dismembered piece, so when investigators finally arrived at the burial plot, only the body of the horse remained, and Carr was not tried for Cobden's murder.

Carr was tried, in Harrison, for the murder of Frankie Osborne, but the jury could not arrive at a verdict and a second trial was scheduled at Ithaca. On Christmas Eve, 1885, Carr was found guilty of manslaughter and was sentenced to fifteen years at hard labor. A year later, however, the Michigan Supreme Court overturned the jury's verdict and ordered Carr released.

Carr spent most of the next two years in jail or courtrooms defending himself against a variety of charges and staying out of jail. But, while always remaining one lucky step ahead of the law, he lost his fortune, and his stockades faded as lumbering operations moved further north to the Upper Peninsula.

For eight tempestuous years, Jim Carr brought entertainment to lumberjacks, was directly or indirectly responsible for several murders, and had accumulated and lost a fortune. On March 15, 1892, 37-year-old Jim Carr, broke and sick, died in a small, cold shanty on a deserted logging road south of Meredith.

THE PERFECT ALIBI
Jackson
January 25, 1889

The following morning, Latimer entered a barbershop without bothering to change his blood-spattered coat and shirt.

Closely linked to lumbering, Michigan's railway system developed in two distinct stages. Before 1860, rail travel was primitive, dangerous, and uncomfortable, and, because of the limited rail accessibility to most cities, passengers usually began and ended their train journey by stagecoach, riverboat, or lake steamer. By 1860, only three major railroads — the Michigan Central, Michigan

Southern, and Detroit and Milwaukee — had laid a mere eight hundred miles of track throughout the Lower Peninsula.

But following the Civil War, Michigan's railroads entered into their "golden age." By 1890, over four thousand miles of track crossed the state and reached nearly every community. Dining and Pullman cars, air brakes, and standard-gauge track made travel convenient and safe. Railroads became not only the major method of freight transportation, but also, the perfect means of mass transit.

For 23-year-old Robert Irving Latimer, the railroad would provide, according to his plan, not only the opportunity to murder but also the perfect alibi.

Latimer devised what he considered to be a simple, yet brilliant plot to murder his sixty-year-old mother so he could inherit the family fortune as well as collect her life insurance. He would, making a great effort to be noticed, travel by train from Jackson to Detroit, sneak back unseen, again by train, to his family's Jackson estate, murder his mother, and surreptitiously take the train back to Detroit. Latimer bungled his great plan from start to finish.

On January 25, 1889, Latimer arrived in Detroit on the train, checked into a hotel, and that evening slipped out a back door in full view of a porter who, because of Latimer's very suspicious movements, carefully noted the strange guest's description. Then, instead of taking an available direct train to Jackson, Latimer boarded a Michigan Central train to Ypsilanti where he transferred to a train to Jackson. By doing so, he risked being identified by two conductors instead of one. And both conductors, as it turned out, did remember Latimer.

Upon reaching the family estate, Latimer locked up the family's small dog (something only a family member could do without the dog barking), killed his mother, and slipped back to the train station. On the "secret" return trip to Detroit, Latimer loudly berated a conductor when he couldn't get a sleeping berth.

The following morning, Latimer entered a barbershop next to his Detroit hotel without bothering to change his blood-spattered coat and shirt. As the barber shaved Latimer, a maid entered the murderer's hotel room to find his bed still perfectly made; he hadn't thought to make it look slept in.

Latimer was arrested, and during the coverage of his trial, a newspaper printed a sketch of Latimer painting a sign reading, "I went this way." Latimer was convicted and sentenced to life imprisonment at the Michigan State Prison. While there, he became a model prisoner and a trustee and eventually took charge of the prison pharmacy. On the night of March 24, 1893, he served two guards a midnight snack of sardines and lemonade spiked with prussic acid and opium. Within twenty minutes, the concoction killed one guard, for which Latimer received another life sentence.

Latimer again became a model prisoner, ironically becoming very popular with the prison guards. After spending forty-six years in prison, Latimer was released in 1935 at the age of sixty-nine. After being picked up as a vagrant a few times, he was placed in a state home for the aged where he died in 1946.

BUSINESS AS USUAL

Aral

August 10, 1889

Marshall scrambled for safety, stared at Wright for several moments, and decided to return to town for help.

In 1889, a few frame houses, a general store, a sawmill on Otter Creek, a schoolhouse, a post office, and two boardinghouses were all that were left of the once busy lumbering town of Aral (which no longer exists) on the shore of Lake Michigan between Frankfort and Empire. By 1886, loggers had removed most of the area's big pine timber and, with most of the town's residents, moved north.

But, under the astute and aggressive management of 38-year-old Charles T. Wright, the town's sawmill still employed two hundred men, who turned out shingles, fence posts, railroad ties, and hardwood for furniture and flooring. Wright, an attractive, successful, and boisterous man, treated his employees fairly and honestly, and they, in turn, adored and respected him. But Wright didn't get along with everyone in the area, and the sheriff had arrested him several times for assault and battery, once for carving up a man's face with a knife.

By summer, 1889, Wright also faced another, more serious, problem with the law. As a result of a quarrel over the amount of taxes he owed Benzie County, Wright had decided to pay none. The court, in turn, had attached the mill's logs and had deputized Neil Marshall and Lake

Township Supervisor Dr. Frank Thurber to confiscate them. Wright had begged the court to attach his finished products rather than the logs, pleading that without logs to saw, he would have to shut the mill down and lay off all his employees. If he could keep the mill open until fall, he argued, he would have enough money to pay his back taxes.

But the court refused, and, on August 10, 1889, a hot Saturday morning, 42-year-old Neil Marshall, at six feet, six inches, and 280 pounds, reputedly the largest man in Benzie County, stood at the foot of a pile of logs and threatened the men at the top with arrest if they rolled another log into the creek. The men looked at Marshall then turned to look at Wright, who, with a hunting rifle on his lap, sat on a log fifty yards away. The burly, barrel-chested Wright wiped sweat from his high-domed, tanned forehead with his sleeve then said calmly, "Don't interfere with my men or I'll drop you where you stand." At that comment, the men on the pile sent one log rolling down and then another. Marshall scrambled to safety, stared at Wright for several moments, and decided to return to town for help.

At the general store, Marshall met 43-year-old Dr. Thurber, who had just returned from a house call. Dr. Thurber, one of the town's most respected and influential men, who, in addition to his medical practice and job as supervisor, also taught school, listened intently as Marshall told what had happened at the mill. Thinking he might be able to reason with Wright, Thurber joined Marshall and, at 2:30 that afternoon, they headed toward the mill.

Charles Wright, who, after his confrontation with Marshall, had walked the streets of Aral while wildly waving his rifle and swigging from a quart whiskey bottle, had returned to the mill and sat chatting with his blacksmith when a voice hollered, "Here they come again." Wright jerked up his rifle, ran toward Otter Creek, and met Marshall and Thurber just after they had crossed a wooden bridge near his log piles.

For a few moments, Wright argued and gestured wildly as he walked beside the two deputies. Suddenly, the mill owner jumped in front of Marshall and raised his rifle. Instinctively, Marshall grabbed the gun just below the muzzle, but Wright jerked it free and shot the huge deputy through the chest just below his heart. Marshall staggered a step or two, groaned loudly, and fell face downward into the dust.

Thurber, grazed by the bullet that had passed completely through Marshall's body, cried, "My God, what have you done!" and grabbed the rifle as Wright furiously tried to lever in another shell. The two men then swayed from side to side for several seconds as they struggled for control of the weapon. About thirty feet from Marshall's body, Thurber finally jerked the rifle free, but, as he did, Wright wrapped his thick left arm around Thurber's neck and pulled his head to his chest. With his right hand, Wright quickly pulled a pistol from his hip pocket, put the barrel into Thurber's ear, and pulled the trigger. Thurber dropped the rifle and fell dead.

Wright calmly walked back to his office, ordered the bodies shaded from the sun with umbrellas, and said to his workers, "Those two crazy fools pitched in to me and I had to shoot them. I feel sorry for them and their families, but they shouldn't have done what they did. A man has a right to protect his own property."

For the next three hours, Wright conducted business as

usual, handed out paychecks to his men, and, at 6:00 p.m., disappeared into the woods. Later that night, a posse captured the mill owner.

Wright was tried, convicted of first-degree murder, and sentenced to life imprisonment at hard labor. Twelve years later, despite the bitter protests of the widows, children, and friends of the slain men, Michigan Governor Hazen Pingree, for reasons never revealed, commuted Wright's sentence and released him.

THE GOGEBIC
STAGECOACH ROBBERY

Lake Gogebic
August 26, 1889

Adolph Fleischbein, a vacationing Belleville, Illinois, banker, settled back with four wealthy Chicago bankers in a Milwaukee, Lakeshore and Western railway stagecoach as they headed from Gogebic Station to a summer resort at Lake Gogebic.

Shortly before noon and two miles from the depot, Reimund (Reinhardt) Holzhey, a 22-year-old, five-foot, seven-inch, Gogebic County train robber, jumped from behind a thicket and, while pointing a revolver at the driver with his right hand, ordered the stage stopped. With his left hand Holzhey waved a second gun at the passengers and, in a thick German accent, said, "Donate; I am collecting."

"Here's my donation," yelled one of the Chicago bankers as he jerked a pistol from his pocket and fired three shots at Holzhey from less than five feet away.

But all three bullets missed, and Holzhey rapidly emptied the chambers of both his revolvers at the passengers. One shot hit Fleischbein in the left thigh and ripped upward into his bowels. The shock and pain caused Fleischbein to stand straight up, and Holzhey sent a second bullet smashing into Fleischbein's hip. Almost simultaneously, the driver whipped the horses which bolted away and flipped Fleischbein off the stagecoach onto the roadway. As the stage drove rapidly away, Holzhey calmly took a ten dollar gold piece, a five dollar bill, and a gold watch from the severely wounded banker's pockets, then disappeared into the woods. Fleischbein bled in the dirt for more than two hours before anyone returned to help him and died at Bessemer the next day.

Railroad officials offered a $1,000 reward for Holzhey's capture and hired Pinkerton's National Detective Agency to join the manhunt. On August 31, 1889, Marshall John Glode captured Holzhey at Republic. Holzhey was tried, convicted, and sentenced to life imprisonment for the murder during, what turned out to be, the last stagecoach robbery in Michigan.

FATAL FEUD

Seney
June 25, 1891

Dan Dunn usually carried out his threats.

In 1881, as thousands of brawling lumberjacks, railroad workers, gamblers, and prostitutes flocked across the Mackinac Straits in a final assault in Michigan's war on virgin timber, the town of Seney was established at the end of an Upper Peninsula logging road. Seney rapidly grew, "like an ugly poisonous toadstool," until, by 1890, the town's wild lawless streets were lined with twenty-one saloons and two monstrous, competing whorehouses, one owned by Dan Dunn and the other by the six Harcourt brothers, Tom, Luke, Jim, Dick, Bill, and Steve.

Dunn and the Harcourts had fought from the time they opened rival saloons in Roscommon and had carried their feud to Seney. Dan Dunn and Tom Harcourt also battled for political control of Seney, and each routinely kept a variety of authorities and officials on their payroll. The feud finally boiled, and Dunn threatened to shoot any Harcourt on sight.

Dunn usually carried out his threats as evidenced by two earlier "problems" he had disposed of. When an old drunk lumberjack whom Dunn had paid to burn his Roscommon saloon for the insurance money showed up in Seney and tried to blackmail him, Dunn took him to an island in the great swamp surrounding Seney and shot the old man in the back. A short time later, a Roscommon druggist demanded repayment of a loan he had made Dunn and ended up in a grave on the same island.

But twenty-year-old Steve Harcourt didn't fear Dan Dunn or his threat and, on June 25, 1891, sauntered casually into Dunn's bar and loudly ordered drinks for all the customers standing at the forty-foot-long polished bar. Dunn glared for a few seconds then coldly said he wouldn't serve "a goddamned Harcourt" a drink in his saloon. Young Harcourt laughed derisively, turned toward the men at the bar, and said, "I'm gonna tell you a few things about this no good bastard." As Harcourt began matter-of-factly listing all of Dunn's past crimes and misdemeanors, Dunn smashed a whiskey bottle over his head.

Steve staggered a few steps, and, as he fumbled for a gun which was wrapped in a red handkerchief in his pocket, Dunn reached under the bar, grabbed his own gun, and shot Harcourt in the mouth. As customers dived for cover, Steve pulled his gun and shot Dunn in the hand, and another shot ricocheted off the top of the bar past Dunn into a picture of John L. Sullivan that hung over an enormous beveled mirror. Gagging on his own blood, Harcourt then backed toward the door, and Dunn shot him again, this time in the stomach. Harcourt, with help, made it to his mother's home where he died three days later.

Dunn was arrested for manslaughter but the charges were dismissed a few days later at a preliminary hearing because, according to Harcourt sympathizers, Dunn had paid off the right county officials and witnesses.

THE LAST STRAW

Trout Lake
July 26, 1891

Dunn saw the brothers come through the door and spun toward them as he reached in his pocket for a gun.

After Dan Dunn was set free, the five remaining Harcourts drew straws to see which brother would execute Steve Harcourt's killer. Jim Harcourt drew the short straw. Upon learning of the Harcourts' desire for revenge, Dunn convinced, or paid, a judge to swear out a peace warrant against the brothers. Dunn then fled to St. Ignace, and the Schoolcraft County Sheriff went to Seney to serve the warrant on the Harcourts.

Surprisingly, the Harcourts offered no resistance and three of the brothers accompanied the arresting officer to a hearing at Manistique. On Sunday, July 26, 1891, at Trout Lake, the sheriff and Harcourts headed for a saloon to spend a 45-minute wait while changing trains.

In an ironic twist of fate, Dan Dunn, also waiting to change trains while on his way from St. Ignace to Manistique as a witness against the Harcourts, stood at the end of the bar. Dunn glanced into the mirror, saw the brothers coming through the door, and spun toward them as he reached in his pocket for a gun. But Jim Harcourt saw the move, whipped out his .32 revolver, shot Dunn through the heart, and fired two more shots into Dunn's body before it hit the saloon's wooden floor. Harcourt then calmly straddled Dunn's body, fired two more shots at, but missed, Dunn's head, and handed his gun to the sheriff.

Jim Harcourt was tried, found guilty of manslaughter, and sentenced to seven and a half years at Marquette Prison. After serving three years of the sentence, he was pardoned and went on to become a township supervisor, deputy sheriff, a conservation officer, and well-respected citizen of Schoolcraft County.

In 1894, lumbering operations moved north to Grand Marais and Seney was all but abandoned.

CONDEMNED

Corunna
May 23, 1893

The mob searched the train, car by car, as a man with a rope walked along the platform.

By 1890, nearly every Michigan community sought access to a rail line since commerce and settlement seemed to follow the tracks. Many towns existed solely because of the railroads. Durand, for example, became the center of Michigan's railroad activity simply because all the state's rail traffic intersected at its depot.

At Durand, shortly before Christmas of 1892, William Sullivan, a 26-year-old drifter, arrived from New Haven, his home town, and loitered around the depot while asking for work. Thirty-five-year-old Layton Leech and his wife of one year felt sorry for Sullivan, whose discolored teeth and scarred neck marred his otherwise harmless, boyish appearance, and charitably hired him to chop wood and do other "make-work" chores at their prosperous farm.

At about six p.m. on New Year's Day, 1893, Leech and Sullivan walked toward a surrounding forest to set snares for a group of rabbits Sullivan had found in an old log. As they passed the barn, Sullivan picked up an axe, buried it in the back of Leech's head, chopped the farmer several more times in the head and face, and dragged the bleeding and mangled victim into the barn. Sullivan took $40 from Leech's pocket then went into the house. There, he beat Mrs. Leech, shot her in the neck, raped her, and, after looting the house, left her for dead. But Mrs. Leech regained consciousness the next morning, crawled through the snow for help, and told of Sullivan's brutal attack.

The stunned community posted a $1,500 reward for Sullivan's capture, and the attention of the entire southern Lower Peninsula focused on the manhunt. After nearly five months and more than forty mistaken sightings of Sullivan around the state, Shiawassee County Sheriff William E. Jacobs finally received the telegram he had been waiting for. New Haven police had positively captured Sullivan practically in his own backyard and asked Jacobs to pick up the prisoner. On May 21, 1893, as Sheriff Jacobs arrived at New Haven, a small group of men congregated at Durand's depot and talked intensely of lynching Sullivan.

Sheriff Jacobs knew he would have problems taking Sullivan through Durand but didn't think he need take any elaborate precautions at New Haven. Expecting only a few curiosity-seekers to gather at the New Haven train station, Jacobs planned to wait behind a freight shed then, after the on-lookers got tired of waiting and left, sneak Sullivan into a freight car. But when more than a hundred noisy people showed up, Jacobs got nervous, forgot his plan, stood on the wrong side of the tracks, and, in full view of the gathered crowd, pushed Sullivan into boxcar No. 21016 on the 10:45 p.m. train.

The growing crowd at Durand suspected that Jacobs would bring Sullivan through on that late train, scheduled to pass through Durand at 3:45 a.m., and, by 11:00 p.m., more than one hundred men waited at the depot. At midnight, the number of the prison boxcar flashed over the wire and the leaderless, but orderly, crowd grew more determined to avenge the murder of their slain neighbor. Jacobs received word of the awaiting crowd and, during a stop at Fenton, secretly moved his frightened prisoner to a sleeper car at the end of the train and locked the doors.

As the train approached the Durand yards, several men with lanterns ran alongside looking for boxcar No. 21016 and, when the train stopped at the station, signaled the location to the rest of the crowd which jumped from the platform, rushed to the car, and pulled the door open. Finding the car empty, the mob then searched the rest of the train, car by car, as a man with a rope walked along the platform. The group finally reached the sleeper car, and, as they tried to force open the doors, the train pulled out of the station. About thirty of the men, including the one with the rope, jumped aboard the moving train as it headed for the county seat, Corunna, eleven miles away.

About three blocks before the Corunna stop, Jacobs and his prisoner suddenly jumped from the slowly moving train and ran toward the jail. The move caught the mob by surprise and Jacobs was able to lock his sweat-drenched prisoner in a cell before the mob reached the jail. At 4:00 a.m., Jacobs turned out the lights, and most of the crowd disappeared.

But by 6:00 a.m., a large crowd was again gathering as people, hoping to get a view of the "brutal fiend," arrived on horses, in wagons, and by train from all over the county. At 8:00 a.m., Jacobs opened the jail and, for the next ten hours, hundreds of curiosity-seekers filed past Sullivan's cell and viewed the accused murderer, who sullenly glared back at them. By 6:00 p.m., five hundred people milled around in front of the jail, and a worn and weary Jacobs locked the doors and stationed thirteen armed deputies throughout the building.

By 9:00 p.m., the mood of the crowd turned menacing as 1,200 howling, hooting people, many arriving from an afternoon in the saloons, screamed, "Let's get him. Let's lynch him." And, out of the sight of the main crowd and the deputies, one hundred men, many of them friends of the murdered farmer, began assembling about two blocks south of the jail. At about 9:30 p.m., this group tied handkerchiefs around their faces and moved slowly toward the jail. One man carried a sledgehammer, another looped a rope with a noose over his shoulder, and five others hoisted a large battering ram. Suddenly, at 9:49 p.m., the jail door flew off its hinges, and the mob stormed inside and quickly overpowered and bound the sheriff and deputies.

The man with the sledgehammer then smashed the lock off Sullivan's cell and another rushed inside with a lantern. For a brief second, the crowd hushed and hesitated. Sullivan lay in a growing pool of blood which gushed from an eight-inch-long, two-inch-deep gash in his neck. The jagged neck of a broken bottle lay next to Sullivan's right hand. Sullivan had ended his own life rather than let the mob tear him apart.*

But that didn't stop the mob. The man with the rope pushed his way into the cell and looped the noose around Sullivan's bloody neck while another kicked viciously at the prisoner's body. A stream of blood marked the trail as the men dragged the body across the stone floor and out the door. From the darkness men rushed to grab the fifty-foot rope, thickly lined themselves along it, and jerked and dragged the rolling, thumping body toward an oak tree a few hundred feet from the jail. The immense cheering crowd went wild, and many stomped on the body as it moved toward the tree.

A young man, rumored to be the murdered man's brother, tossed the end of the rope over a limb, and scores of hands grabbed it and, with a sudden jerk, pulled the body from the ground. With a swerve, Sullivan's body wrapped around the trunk then dangled in the dim light while people kicked, punched, pulled, and even knifed it. The original lynchers then fled, but the remaining mob lowered the body and ripped off all the clothes before raising it again.

When the mob lowered the mutilated body for the

---

* Others later claimed that members of the mob staged the "suicide" so they would not be charged with murder as a result of the lynching.

final time and removed the rope, two hundred boys, some as young as ten, dragged it up and down the streets, over rough pavement, and through mud puddles. As they did, the adults cut the rope, tree limb, and Sullivan's clothes into small pieces and passed them out as souvenirs. Sheriff Jacobs finally broke free but arrived only in time to prevent the boys from burning Sullivan's body in front of the saloon.

No charges were ever filed against the "unidentified" lynchers, and, within two weeks, press coverage of the incident stopped.

I DONE MY DUTY

Buffalo, New York
September 6, 1901

As Czolgosz fell into single file, he reached into his pocket for his revolver.

At the turn of the century, industrialization brought rapid change to Michigan and America. Rapid growth of cities generated overcrowding, lack of proper sanitation, and inadequate police and fire protection. Society became conventionalized and institutionalized, and large corporations seemed to manipulate economic and political power without regard for the welfare of the general public. And workers felt that they were being exploited in a frenzied quest for wealth by the barons of big industry.

Amid this atmosphere of social and economic upheaval, many Americans felt threatened, and two political reform movements, "progressivism" and "anarchism" took root. Progressives, who came from both the Democratic and Republican parties, called for increased *regulation* of business, better protection for workers, and popular control over all phases of government. Radical anarchists, on the other hand, advocated the total *elimination* of government, elected officials, corporations, voting, marriage, and all other institutions. On September 6, 1901, Leon F. Czolgosz, a young, Michigan-born farmhand and factory worker, put the anarchist philosophy into violent practice and changed the course of U.S. history.

In 1873, a few months after his parents arrived from Poland, Czolgosz was born in Detroit, the fourth of eight children. His family moved often — to Rogers City in 1879, Posen in 1879, Alpena in 1884, Pittsburgh, Pennsylvania, in 1889, and Cleveland, Ohio, in 1891.

As an adult, the outwardly calm and non-violent Czolgosz churned on the inside. The hardships endured by his Polish immigrant family, forcing their constant relocation, caused him to hate America and embrace first socialism then anarchism. When, on July 29, 1900, a Pattern, New Jersey, anarchist traveled to Monza, Italy, and assassinated King Humbert I, Czolgosz was so fascinated that, for weeks, he took the newspaper account of the killing to bed with him. Czolgosz quit his factory job and, for the next year, wandered aimlessly between Cleveland, Fort Wayne, Indiana, and Chicago, attending a few anarchist meetings and lectures.

On August 31, 1901, Czolgosz traveled to Buffalo, New York, site of the Pan-American Exposition, and, under the name John Doe, paid $2 in advance for a week's rental of a room over a saloon. The next day, Czolgosz bought a .32 caliber Iver Johnson revolver, whose hard rubber handle had an owl's head stamped on both sides, then spent the next five days in his room reading newspapers.

On the morning of September 6, Czolgosz arose early, eager to perform what he had planned to be an act of duty. Dressed neatly in a striped gray suit, flannel shirt, string tie, and cap, he tucked his revolver into his right hip pocket, had breakfast, went to a barbershop for a shave, and took a relaxing excursion to Niagara Falls. Upon returning to Buffalo in the early afternoon, Czolgosz went to the site of the Pan-American Exposition and joined a line of people waiting outside the Temple of Music in which, in an hour, President William McKinley would hold a ten-minute reception.

At 4:00 p.m., the door opened and the line of people began to move toward the president. Five minutes later Czolgosz entered the door, sixty-four feet from the president. Two lines of policemen and soldiers gradually narrowed, funneling the people two abreast, then single file, toward the president. As Czolgosz fell into single file, sixteen feet from McKinley, he reached into his pocket for his revolver. On the hot and humid day, many people in the line mopped sweat from their brows, so no one paid any attention when he drew his revolver and wrapped a large white handkerchief around it and his right hand, which he then held tightly against his side as if injured.

At 4:07 p.m., as low strains of a Bach sonata throbbed through the temple, Czolgosz stepped in front of McKinley. McKinley thrust out his hand, but Czolgosz slapped it aside, lunged forward, and fired twice through the handkerchief, setting it on fire. Powder stained McKinley's white vest as one bullet bounced off his breastbone and the other ripped into his abdomen, perforating the front and rear of his stomach and lodging in his back muscles, never to be found. Shivering, the president straightened up to his full height, looked at Czolgosz in astonishment, and slumped into the arms of the men around him.

Immediately, eight or nine soldiers knocked Czolgosz down, fell on him, and beat the five-foot, seven-inch, 140-pound man with their fists and rifles. As he was beaten, Czolgosz muttered, "I done my duty." One of the soldiers prepared to stab Czolgosz with his bayonet, but McKinley, who had not lost consciousness, called out, "Be easy with him, boys," and Secret Service agents quickly rushed the assailant out of the room. McKinley lived for eight days, and, with his death, Theodore Roosevelt, at forty-two, became the youngest president in the nation's history.

On September 23, four days after McKinley's funeral, Czolgosz was put on trial. After an 8½-hour trial, during which neither Czolgosz nor his reluctant court-appointed attorneys offered any defense, the jury convicted him of murder in the first degree, and the judge sentenced him to be electrocuted.

At 7:12 a.m. on October 29, the warden of the New York Penitentiary in Auburn led Czolgosz to the electric chair. As guards bound the chair's straps around him, Czolgosz said, "I killed the president because he was an enemy of the good people — of the working people." The assassin then stiffened as 1,700 volts of electricity surged through his body. At 7:17 a.m., he was pronounced dead.

A prison burial detail then removed the body of 28-year-old Czolgosz, still bruised and lacerated from the beatings of police, soldiers, and prison guards, to the prison cemetery. After lowering the corpse into an unmarked grave, the detail poured a carboy of acid into the hole, and, twelve hours later, Leon F. Czolgosz's body disintegrated.

I HATE
THE LITTLE BRAT

Clare
June 19, 1902

"What have you done to my baby!" Mrs. Paradie screamed.

In September, 1902, thirteen-year-old Anna Curtis stood before a judge and jury in Harrison as the youngest child in Michigan, at that time, ever to be accused of murder.

Anna's parents ran a boardinghouse on Clare's West Seventh Street, and, in May, 1902, George Paradie, his wife, and thirteen-month-old son, Fennal, moved in. The Paradies and Curtises got along well, except for Anna, who intensely disliked the baby. In mid-June, as Anna pulled and jerked Fennal down the street in her wagon, a passing neighbor remarked how cute the baby was, and Anna snapped, "I hate the little brat. I'm going to kill it."

During the pleasant late afternoon of June 19, 1902, Mrs. Curtis and Mrs. Paradie chatted amiably as they cleaned strawberries on the boardinghouse's porch when, suddenly, Fennal screamed. Both women rushed to his crib and recoiled at the sight of Fennal's horribly burned mouth, face, and neck. As Mrs. Curtis screamed for someone to get a doctor, Anna appeared in the doorway. "What have you done to my baby!" Mrs. Paradie screamed, but Anna just looked blankly at her and said nothing. The doctor arrived but could do nothing. Someone had poured carbolic acid into Fennal's mouth, and, as his frantic mother helplessly watched, the unconscious baby jerked spastically in a neighbor's lap until dying an hour later.

Anna was arrested two days later and tried at Harrison in September, 1902. During the trial, Anna's father admitted he had purchased a bottle of carbolic acid at the drugstore the Saturday before Fennal's death, and it had disappeared. Anna's Sunday-school teacher said she had seen Anna with a bottle of carbolic acid. A housekeeper told the jury that she had found a partially empty bottle of carbolic acid in the Curtises' woodshed the day after the poisoning. And Mrs. Paradie testified that the only people in the Curtis home from the time she put Fennal in his crib until the time she discovered her mutilated baby were herself, Mrs. Curtis, and Anna.

But Anna's defense attorney argued that all the evidence was circumstantial and also pleaded, "A child who is so young is not capable of forcing an intent to commit a crime of this magnitude. She is only a little girl, not yet fourteen, and, in the eyes of the law, she is innocent."

On September 15, 1902, the jury found Anna not guilty.

MARY LIKED TO GO TO FUNERALS

Fife Lake
May 2, 1903

Mary Murphy wept as her tormented brother opened his eyes and cried, "Hold me down, Joe, my feet will come up."

Mary Murphy, a kind, friendly and gentle person, loved to dress up for social occasions. And few social occasions in backwoods Michigan at the turn of the century equaled a funeral. A funeral, often the only affair that brought an entire family together, was usually followed by an almost festive wake that gave hardworking farmers an excuse to relax and their wives a chance to dress up.

Mary Murphy seemed to enjoy going to funerals, and death hung on the black taffeta dress, black hat, and veil she wore so many times. By the time she arrived in Fife Lake in 1899, she had already attended a sorrowfully impressive list of funerals. Mary's first husband, James Ambrose, died suddenly in 1887, and she also buried all her children from that marriage — three who died in infancy and two who died of diptheria at ages five and seventeen. Shortly after Ambrose's death, Mary married Ernest McKnight, and in 1889, the couple moved from Alpena to Grayling. Mary's father died in 1894, and, in 1898, second husband Ernest died.

After Ernest's death, Mary sold their property, moved in with her mother and a mentally retarded niece at the family's Fife Lake farm, and added to the funeral list. In late winter, 1903, Mary's brother John, his wife Gertrude, and three-month-old baby daughter moved into the farmhouse while John built a new house nearby. On Monday, April 24, 1903, Gertrude left the baby with Mary, a trained nurse and midwife, and went to help John at the house. When the young couple returned later that afternoon, Mary sobbed that the baby had tragically died of sudden spasms. John consoled the two grief-stricken women for several minutes then left for town to buy a small coffin. When he returned five hours later, Mary tearfully told him that Gertrude had died of an epileptic fit brought on by the baby's death.

A little more than a week later, on a cold and blustery May 2, John Murphy lay on his back across his bed, his twitching legs protruding stiffly from his gray flannel nightgown. Sweat rolled over his closed eyelids and down his red face, and foam bubbled from the corners of his mouth. Joe Battenfield, a friend and neighbor who had been summoned by John's mother, moved to John's side and moved an open bottle of camphor under the stricken man's nose. Mary Murphy wept as her tormented brother opened his eyes and cried, "Hold me down, Joe, my feet will come up." Battenfield pressed his knees against Murphy's legs, and John's body twitched and heaved uncontrollably for two more agonizing minutes before he mercifully died.

The sympathetic and kind folks of Springfield Township felt that three deaths in a little more than a week was more than any family should have to bear. So did a suspicious Grand Traverse County prosecutor, E.C. Smith, who ordered John's body exhumed and sent the dead man's organs to Ann Arbor for analysis. A week later the report came back: the strychnine found in John's stomach would have killed ten men.

Smith then launched a thorough investigation into Mary Murphy's past and compiled an appalling report:

—James Ambrose, Mary's first husband, died in agony, his limbs twitching convulsively.

—Mrs. McKnight, the first wife of Mary's second husband Ernest, died in Alpena, in July, 1887, after experiencing severe convulsions while under Mary's care.

—Two days after Mrs. McKnight's death, Mary's niece, baby Teeple, also died of convulsions while under Mary's care.

—In Grayling, after drinking tea with Mary in May, 1892, Eliza Chalker, another niece, foamed at the mouth and died.

— Nine months later, also in Grayling, Sarah Murphy, Mary's sister, died, also after drinking tea with Mary.

— Ernest McKnight, Mary's second husband, drove his wagon to cut some hay and, shortly after eating a lunch prepared by Mary, became violently ill but made it home. By the next morning, he had recovered, but that night, Mary reported, he died in his sleep.

— In 1896, Mrs. Carey, a relative of Mary's, mysteriously died.

— Dorothy Jensen, a child in the care of Mary, died on Good Friday, 1902, after uncontrollably twitching and foaming at the mouth.

Prosecutor Smith added the names of John, Gertrude, and baby Murphy to the horrifying report and continued his investigation. He ordered the bodies of Gertrude and the baby exhumed, and the Ann Arbor medical examiner found large amounts of strychnine in both. A neighbor, present when the baby died, told Smith she had seen Mary give the baby a pill shortly before it went into spasms and died. Shortly after that, according to the same witness, Mary gave Gertrude a pill for her nerves, and Gertrude immediately fell to the floor, her limbs twitching horribly until she died.

Smith arrested Mary, and she admitted that she had given her brother and his family homemade strychnine-quinine pills but only to soothe, not kill, them.

Forty-year-old Mary Murphy McKnight was tried, found guilty of murder in the first degree of her brother John, and sentenced to life imprisonment. She spent eighteen years in the Detroit House of Corrections before being paroled.

AN UNPARDONABLE
PARDON

Bad Axe
1909-1911

The new automobile attracted a lot of attention to its owner and fueled gossip about an affair between Dr. MacGregor and Carrie Sparling.

The people of Bad Axe labeled the family, the "dying Sparlings" and attributed their strange symptoms and untimely deaths to the "will of God."

John Wesley Sparling, a 46-year-old, up-to-date, hard-working, and highly respected farmer, died first. During haying season in July, 1909, John, who had never been sick a day in his life, suddenly left the field extremely ill and went to the house where his beautiful wife Carrie and daughter May helped him into bed. John spent the next week in bed, vomiting and in agony, before he died.

After John's death, 25-year-old Peter, the oldest of John's four educated, strapping, churchgoing sons, took charge of the farm work, and Carrie, with the helpful advice of the family physician, Dr. John MacGregor, did all the planning and decision-making. A year passed, haying time came again, and the Sparling fields were lined with long windrows of drying clover. Almost exactly a year after his father's death, Peter staggered from the field to the house and died five days later. Albert, the next oldest Sparling, became the nominal head of the farm, but in May, 1911, he became ill at church and, after suffering the exact symptoms as Peter and his father, died.

At the bedside of each Sparling during his ordeal sat compassionate Dr. John MacGregor. Six months before John Sparling's mysterious illness and death, MacGregor had begun the first of many visits to the farm to treat Carrie for a persistent eye infection. MacGregor's kindness during her husband's illness so moved Carrie Sparling that, after her husband's death, she appointed the doctor the official family advisor. MacGregor, six feet tall, thirty-six years old, handsome, and married, called on beautiful Carrie nearly every day which, at first, caused no undue gossip around Bad Axe since widows in that place and time often leaned on the family doctor for advice.

A month after her husband John's death, MacGregor advised Carrie to insure the lives of her four sons for $1,000 each. MacGregor, as the examining physician, certified that the boys were in excellent health, and MacGregor's father, an insurance agent in Canada, wrote the policies. Six months later, Carrie took out a second set of policies in the same manner.

When Peter died, Carrie bought a comfortable cottage in the nearby village of Ubly with the insurance proceeds and let MacGregor and his wife live there rent-free. After Albert's death, Carrie endorsed over the life insurance check to MacGregor who then purchased an automobile. The fantastic novelty, a rare sight in Huron County at the time, attracted a lot of attention to its owner and fueled gossip about an affair between Dr. MacGregor and Carrie Sparling. MacGregor drove to the farm daily and, in long conferences with Carrie, became the active director of the farm, telling the beautiful widow when to plow, plant, and sell livestock.

Then, on a warm, sticky August 4, 1911, the strange symptoms of the "dying Sparlings" struck a third Sparling son, Scyrel. Heat waves shimmered up and down the Sparling barn as the thresher's mechanical beaters rhythmically thumped on the yellow oats. Rugged Scyrel, the strongest man in the crew, worked hard as usual but noticed, before noon, that no oat dust stuck to his face; he wasn't sweating. Shortly after, he staggered to the house and began vomiting uncontrollably.

For some unknown reason, perhaps because of the gossip circulating about him and Carrie or to protect his medical reputation (three patients mysteriously dying within two years might have raised doubts about his ability), MacGregor called in two outside physicians for help. One, Dr. Conboy, immediately went to Huron County's prosecuting attorney, Xenophon Boomhower, and said, "I am certain that Scyrel Sparling is suffering from arsenic poisoning."

Boomhower, an old friend of MacGregor, asked the doctor to arrange for a nurse to stay with Scyrel at all times, and no one, except Dr. MacGregor, was to visit Sparling or give him food, water, or medicine. But, in spite of these precautions, Scyrel grew worse and died on August 14, 1911.

Boomhower ordered Scyrel's organs sent to the University of Michigan where pathologists reported finding arsenic. Boomhower then ordered Albert's body exhumed and examined by the same experts who reported identical findings: death by arsenic poisoning. On January 12, 1912, Boomhower charged MacGregor with the murder of Scyrel Sparling and brought him to trial on April 12.

Boomhower contended that MacGregor had systematically poisoned all four Sparlings to collect, through Carrie, the farm and life insurance money. MacGregor's only defense was the claim that the Sparling men were addicted to patent medicines that contained arsenic. But experts pointed out that such medicines contained too little arsenic to cause death, and the jury found MacGregor guilty of murder in the first degree. MacGregor was sentenced to life imprisonment and, after unsuccessful appeals to the State Supreme Court, entered Jackson prison.

Then, in one of the strangest moves in Michigan judicial and penal history, Governor Woodbridge Ferris, claiming he had irrefutable evidence of MacGregor's innocence, granted a full and unconditional pardon in November, 1916. Whatever evidence Ferris had, he did not reveal nor has it been revealed to this day. Ferris followed his remarkable pardon with two more extraordinary actions. First, Ferris brought MacGregor to Lansing and gave him his pardon personally and, second, Ferris appointed MacGregor as the official state doctor to the prison where he had just been an inmate. In 1928, still the prison doctor, MacGregor died.

TINY WHITE COFFINS

Calumet
December 24, 1913

The piano player leaped from the stage, ran toward the man, and, while another woman calmed the uneasy children, told him to be quiet, that there was no fire.

Immediately following the Civil War, Houghton, Keweenaw, and Ontonagon counties rose to the pinnacle of U.S. copper mining, often producing 200 million pounds a year worth $57 million. The prosperous area attracted so many people that, for a brief time, the Keweenaw Peninsula became the third most densely populated area in Michigan with 95,000 people; only Detroit (465,000) and Grand Rapids (112,000) were bigger.

But, in 1867, Keweenaw County was mined out and, by 1890, so was the Ontonagon River Range. Only mines in the Portage Lake area continued to operate after 1900, and, faced with stiff competition from newly discovered deposits in the West, Michigan fell to third place in copper production. In 1913, the bubble of prosperity and goodwill finally burst, and, during the next year, tragedy and murder shook the copper country.

At the beginning of that year, efficiency became the watchword in the mines, and the pressure for increased production created resentment among the Finnish, Slovenian, Croatian, Italian, and other immigrant miners. Weary of the low wages, long hours, and dangerous working conditions, the miners grew more and more receptive to unionization efforts. Finally, on July 23, 1913, 15,000 copper miners, demanding a $3 minimum daily wage, an eight-hour workday, and recognition of the Western Federation of Miners as their bargaining agent, walked off their jobs and picketed all the major shafts in the copper country.

The strike began peacefully with the miners and their families, dressed in their "Sunday best," marching from the union hall to the picket lines each day, but trouble soon erupted. Strikers intimidated or attacked Cornish supervisors and unsympathetic workers who tried crossing the picket lines. By the end of July, the mining companies and law enforcement officials had hired the New York-based Waddell-Mahon firm, which specialized in supplying armed strikebreakers recruited from New York's slums. At about the same time, Michigan Governor Woodbridge Ferris ordered the entire 2,500-man Michigan National Guard to active duty in the copper country. Even the most non-militant strikers flared at the sight of armed New York City thugs and gunmen driving up and down their streets and militia setting up tents on company property.

The National Guardsmen, for the most part, got along well with the local residents, but the Waddell-Mahon men did not. On August 14, six Waddell-Mahon men and Houghton County deputies, after unsuccessfully attempting to arrest strikers living at a Painesdale boardinghouse, surrounded the house and fired indiscriminately into it. Their bullets killed two Croatian miners and grazed a baby.

By late November, the community was rapidly and violently dividing into two factions. People who felt the strikers had no right to stop the workers from crossing picket lines organized into the Citizens Alliance and wore buttons denoting their organization. Supporters of the strikers, on the other hand, hostilely objected to the companies' policy of importing strikebreakers to work the mines. During the early hours of December 7, three unidentified men fired twelve shots through the windows of a Painesdale boardinghouse where Cornish "strikebreaking" miners stayed. The bullets killed three men in the beds where they slept. The murders galvanized the loosely knit Citizens Alliance, split the community almost asunder, and set up the greatest murder of the strike.

Shortly after dark on Christmas Eve, 1913, hundreds of the striking miners' children eagerly tramped through the deep snow to Calumet's Italian Hall to hear music, see Santa Claus, and open small gifts. The Women's Auxiliary of the striking union had organized the party, obtained donated clothing, candy, and other gifts from unions in far-off cities, and arranged for a local Santa to distribute them. The children, some accompanied by their mothers, filed up a narrow stairway to the second floor, walked through a long cloakroom, and entered the hall. The children then seated themselves at folding tables and chairs and ate Christmas cookies and milk while a lady played Christmas songs on a piano on a small stage at the front of the hall.

More than six hundred people had crammed into the hall by the time the entertainment began. A small girl, wearing a pink ballet skirt and tights, danced around the stage while the candles on a Christmas tree flickered behind her. Other children recited Christmas poems or sang songs. The Santa Claus jumped onto the stage, and the adults organized the excited children into a line which moved along one side of the hall toward the stage.

To the strains of more Christmas music, each wide-eyed child moved up the stage steps, walked to Santa, and received a greeting and gift.

Suddenly, a large man, wearing a long dark overcoat with a fur collar turned up around his face (and said by some, but never proved, to be wearing a Citizens Alliance button) rushed into the hall and yelled, "Fire! Fire!" The piano player leaped from the stage, ran toward the man, and, while another woman calmed the uneasy children, told him to be quiet, that there was no fire. Then, in an effort to help calm the children, she ran back to the stage and began playing the piano again. The man shouted, "Fire! Fire!" again and disappeared out the doorway.

A wave of panic-stricken children and adults swept after him, rushed through the doorway, and jammed into the narrow corridor. A man who stood by the door to insure that only strikers' children came to the party tried to slow the rush, but the wave of children swept over him. Children tripped and fell, their bodies became stumbling blocks for others, and, within seconds, layers of bodies jammed the stairway. Double doors at the bottom of the stairwell opened outward, but the crush of people coming down had wedged the bodies into an immovable wall a few feet from the exit. Back in the hall, children who couldn't get through the jammed doorway scurried around the room like terrified animals. Two crawled out a back window and fell to their deaths.

Someone had pulled the fire alarm, and the fire chief raced from the station, only a block away, pulled open the lower doors, and reeled unbelievingly at the pile of more than one hundred bodies, reaching halfway up to the ceiling, that squirmed a few feet from him. A six-year-old girl at the bottom of the heap reached for him and whimpered, "Help me." But the chief could not pull her out and the little girl closed her eyes while, next to her, a four-year-old, in his last breath gasped, "Mommy."

As those at the bottom of the heap of piled-up bodies slowly died of suffocation, firemen arrived, put ladders to the upstairs windows to enter, and began frantically pulling children off the top of the pile. Hands, legs, and arms were so entangled that it took nearly an hour to sort through the pile of dead and moaning victims. When the firemen finally finished their gruesome task, the bodies of thirty-seven little girls, nineteen small boys, thirteen mothers, and five men lay on the decorated tables in the hall.

Parents, attracted by the town's fire siren and commotion, rushed to the make-shift morgue in search of their children. One mother reached her daughter who was sitting in a chair. The little girl weakly asked, "Mommy, can I have a drink of water?" then slumped over dead. On the table in front of her, still in her pink costume, lay the lifeless body of the little ballet dancer.

On Sunday after Christmas, Calumet's churches conducted mass funeral services for the victims. At the conclusion of the services, the mourners converged at a road junction adjacent to the churches and placed the caskets of the adult dead in several hearses and funeral wagons. Then, with snow slowly falling, the fathers and brothers of the dead children picked up the identical tiny white coffins and walked two miles over snow-covered roads to the cemetery. There, most of the victims were placed in two mass graves, one Catholic, the other Protestant.

The drive toward unionization died with the innocent victims at the Italian Hall, and, by April, the strike officially ended. The Western Federation of Miners ceased to exist in the area, and efforts to unionize did not resume for nearly thirty years.

THE SPY WHO LOVED –
AND MURDERED – WOMEN
Royal Oak
March 17, 1918

A neighbor saw Schmidt cover his basement windows with newspaper and heard a woman crying.

On April 19, 1917, Congress declared war on Germany, and a wave of anti-German sentiment swept across Michigan and the rest of the country. German foods such as sauerkraut and frankfurters were renamed "liberty cabbage" and "hot dogs." Many Michigan residents with German names Americanized them, and the residents of Berlin, Michigan, changed their town's name to the more suitable "Marne." Seized with the fear that the enemy might be close at hand, Michigan residents considered anything even remotely connected with Germany to be suspicious and evil.

In March, 1918, police began receiving reports, from several sources, of suspicious activity at the home of Herman Schmidt, a factory worker with a heavy German accent, who with his wife Helen and seventeen-year-old daughter Gertrude had moved to Royal Oak only months before the declaration of war. A Detroit boardinghouse owner told police this story: In September, 1917, a young lady named Augusta Steinbach rented a room after coming from New York City to marry a Royal Oak man named Herman Neugebauer. Several months later, she checked out and left a forwarding address that turned out to be Schmidt's. In early March, 1918, a wedding present arrived at the boardinghouse, and, when the owner brought it to Schmidt's address, a woman who answered the door said she knew no Augusta Steinbach. Confused, the boardinghouse owner checked with an express agent who verified that Steinbach's trunks had been delivered to the same address.

At about the same time, a New York City girlfriend of Augusta Steinbach's asked a Detroit acquaintance to look up Steinbach and Neugebauer at an address Steinbach had told her was that of her fiance. When the Detroit woman reported back that the man who lived at the address was named Schmidt, was married, and had a seventeen-year-old daughter, the worried friend notified police.

A neighbor told police that, on March 17, he saw Schmidt cover his basement windows with newspaper and heard a woman crying. An hour later, said the same neighbor, thick smoke poured from Schmidt's chimney, and the air was filled with a foul, unusual smell.

On April 22, 1918, police arrested Herman, Gertrude, and Helen and thoroughly searched their home. Police found bloodstained women's clothes under the porch, a bloodstained cleaver buried in the yard, what appeared to be a human bone in an ash pile, and nearly a hundred pieces of women's jewelry hidden around the house. The authorities also determined that Schmidt was registered as an enemy alien and called Department of Justice officials into the investigation. Together they discovered that Augusta Steinbach was not the first woman connected with Schmidt to have mysteriously disappeared.

Herman Schmidt had left a trail of marriages, missing and abandoned women, and murder. Schmidt first came to America in 1913 with his young daughter Gertrude a few years after his wife, Gertrude's mother Anna, mysteriously disappeared. Schmidt settled in Lakewood, New Jersey, where he advertised in a newspaper for a wife. Adele Ulrich answered the ad, married Schmidt in early 1914, and disappeared shortly after. Later that year, in New York City, Schmidt, using the alias Emil Braun, met and married another woman through another matrimonial ad. Mrs. Braun told investigators that "Emil wrote me the most wonderfully worded letters after I answered his ad for a wife, and, when I met him, I was greatly attracted to him. He had a fascinating personality. All women were fond of him.

"Before I became his wife, his daughter Gertrude lived with me at my home by his expressed wish. She spied on me constantly. She was always a designing, deceitful, tattling girl, and I never trusted her. She told her father of every move I made, especially if I went to draw certain amounts of money from the bank."

Mrs. Braun also claimed that Schmidt was a cog in the underground machine of the German Secret Service. She had, she said, discovered letters written from the German

War Office in code and had watched Schmidt sketch the fortifications in New York City's harbor.

Schmidt abandoned Braun, went to Chicago, married another woman in 1915, and left a few days later with $2,000 of her money.

Later that year, Schmidt moved to a house in Highland Park and, while there, placed an ad for a housekeeper in *Staats-Zeitung*, a New York German newspaper. Irma Pallatinus answered the ad and moved into Schmidt's Highland Park home. A year later, just before Schmidt moved to Royal Oak, Pallatinus was strangled with a cord, wrapped in canvas, and buried in the basement of the German's Highland Park home.

In Royal Oak, Schmidt continued his mail-order romances and, after another correspondence courtship, married Helen Tietz of New York. While still married to Helen, Schmidt began a secret correspondence with Augusta Steinbach that eventually brought her and the police to his Royal Oak home.

The day after his arrest, Schmidt confessed that, under the alias Herman Neugebauer, he had lured Augusta to Detroit after a correspondence courtship and proposal. On March 17, 1918, he sent his wife and daughter to the movies, he said, brought Augusta to his home, and told her that he was already married. She was so distraught, he claimed, that she drank poison in his presence, and when she died, he cut up her body, burned it, threw her bloodstained clothing under the porch, and kept all of her jewelry and money.

Schmidt also denied that he was a spy but said he was intimate with those who were and hinted that he would reveal some dramatic information if the officers would leave him alone for just a few moments. The police agreed and left him kneeling, apparently in prayer, on the floor of his jail cell. As soon as the officers left the room, Schmidt released a heavy iron bed folded against the wall, grasped it with both hands, tipped back his head, and, with all his strength, pulled the sharp iron edge against his forehead. When police officers returned to the cell, Schmidt lay dead on the floor, blood and brain tissue oozing from a jagged six-inch gash in his forehead.

It was the code of the Prussian spy, said Mrs. Emil Braun, not fear of the consequences of the death of Augusta Steinbach that drove him to suicide.

THE MODEL T MURDER

Detroit
July, 1923

Kathleen had diligently scrimped and saved and bitterly objected when Frank announced that he was going to spend her entire savings on the frivolous novelty.

In 1896, Ransom E. Olds founded the state's first automobile company, drove the first car down the streets of Lansing, and designed, produced, and advertised automobiles for use by the general public. Others tried to copy Olds' success and, by 1907, 2,700 car-manufacturing companies had sprung up throughout Michigan.

Few survived, but one that did, the Ford Motor Company, directed by the legendary Henry Ford, grew to dominate the industry. Ford stressed durability and dependability in his cars and, by sophisticating and perfecting assembly-line techniques, put the automobile within financial reach of the workingman and farmer. And, because of Ford's fair treatment of his employees, laborers throughout the nation praised him as the only automobile manufacturer with a heart.

After introducing the Model T, the "farmer's car," Ford controlled over half the automobile sales market, selling 1,871,891 vehicles in 1923 alone. A few critics warned that in this frenzy to own an automobile, individual and societal values were being distorted. But few listened, and Americans rushed to Ford dealers at the rate of over 250 per hour.

Frank Gorka was a Detroiter who was swept up in the national mania to own a Model T, and, when he excitedly announced to his family that he planned to buy the vehicle, his wife Kathleen objected bitterly. For years, Kathleen had diligently scrimped and saved so that their family could buy their own home, and now Frank planned to spend her entire savings, $300, on a frivolous novelty. After a heated argument, Frank took the money, left the house, bought a Model T, and returned with the vehicle. The argument continued, and when Frank threatened to take the car and leave his wife and three children, Kathleen shot him dead.

Several days later, as his yacht drifted about Grand

Traverse Bay, Henry Ford looked up from a newspaper account of the shooting and, with tears in his eyes, went to the boat's wireless room. "Tell my office in Dearborn," Ford instructed the radio operator, "to supply bail in any amount and let that woman out of jail." Ford representatives in Detroit rushed to the prosecuting attorney's office but found that friends had already freed Mrs. Gorka under a $10,000 bond.

OPENING THE DOOR

Detroit
September 9, 1925

For the first time in my life, I stood face to face with the same mob that has haunted my people throughout history.

The swift growth of Michigan's automobile industry created a frothing turbulence in its wake of rapid and uncontrolled urbanization. From 1900 through 1925, immigrants, blacks, and southern whites flooded into southern Michigan's industrial towns and cities in search of jobs in the booming economy. As the converging streams met head-on, bitterness grew between the races, and the Ku Klux Klan became increasingly active, spreading through Flint, Saginaw, Bay City, Lansing, Kalamazoo, Muskegon, and the conservative Dutch communities along Lake Michigan.

And Detroit, focal point of the automotive industry and industrialization, also became the center of Klan activity. By 1925, Detroit, which had tripled its population from 1900 to 1920 and had the highest rate of black immigration in the nation, claimed half of Michigan's 80,000 Klan members. The Detroit Klan organized neighborhood "improvement associations" to prevent (violently if necessary) well-to-do blacks from moving into white neighborhoods. During the summer of 1925, rampaging white improvement associations drove six black families out of white Detroit neighborhoods.

On September 8, 1925, members of an east-side Detroit "improvement association" repeatedly phoned Dr. Ossian Sweet and threatened the black physician and his family with violence and death if they did not immediately leave their newly purchased house in an all-white neighborhood. But Sweet, the 31-year-old handsome grandson of an Alabama slave, had struggled for nearly twenty years to arrive at his new $18,500, two-story home and wasn't about to give it up without a fight. Sweet, the oldest of ten children, had worked his way through Wilberforce Academy in Ohio and Howard University Medical School in Washington, D.C. After practicing medicine for several years in Detroit, he studied gynecology and pediatrics in Vienna and in Paris, where he worked at the Curie Institute under Madame Curie herself. After returning to Detroit, Sweet and his light-skinned wife, Gladys, selected their new home and had moved in that night. The Sweets tried to ignore the telephoned threats but spent the first night in their new home afraid to go to sleep.

Late the next afternoon, as an angry group of whites congregated in a school yard across the street from Sweet's home, one of Sweet's brothers and six friends, all armed, joined Ossian and Gladys. By 6:00 p.m., the crowd had grown so large that the six policemen who had maintained order during the day summoned reserves from the station house, and traffic became so heavy that two policemen were detailed to direct and control it. By 8:00 p.m., unruly members of the mob began throwing rocks at the house, and police did nothing to stop them. The Sweets and their friends were nervously playing a game of cards when the first rock hit the roof of the house.

Sweet ran to the window and looked out at a mob of more than seven hundred screaming, rock-throwing whites. Cars had rolled in and parked in every direction, and men, women and children filled the school yard and street and climbed onto porches and rooftops. Sweet reeled in shock, ran to his wife in the kitchen, and snapped off the lights. After quietly and slowly opening the back door, he heard voices outside hoarsely whisper, "Go and raise hell in front; I'll cover the back." Frightened, he grabbed a gun, ran upstairs, and, as rocks clattered against the house, lay trembling on a bed for a few moments.

Suddenly, a rock crashed through the window and flying glass struck Sweet. The doctor ran down the stairs and joined his terrified wife, brother, and friends, who frantically ran from room to room. A car screeched up to the curb, and another Sweet brother, Otis, and a friend jumped out and scrambled toward the house as the mob threw rocks at them and yelled, "They're niggers. Get them! Get the niggers!"

As the two black men rushed toward the house, the mob surged forward and a rock smashed another window. "When I opened the door to let (my brother and friend) in," said Sweet later, "I realized that for the first time in my life I stood face to face with the same mob that has haunted my people throughout its entire history. I knew that my back was against the wall, that I was black and that because I was black and had found the courage to buy a home, they were ready to wreak their vengeance upon me."

But, suddenly, a shot rang out from an upstairs window. The crowd scattered as ten more shots quickly cracked and popped from the windows of the darkened house; then the shooting abruptly stopped. Across the street, Leon Breiner, who had smoked his pipe on a friend's porch while watching the mob, lay dead with a bullet in his back. Police arrested everyone in the house and charged them with the first-degree murder of Breiner.

A committee of the National Association for the Advancement of Colored People (NAACP) hired famous attorney Clarence Darrow to defend the Sweets, and his eloquent defense drew national attention to the NAACP's fight for black civil rights. Darrow built his case on the doctor's fear of the white mob and his right to defend his family. Referring to the precedent-setting case, *People v. Augustus Pond* (see p. 71), Darrow said that Sweet was ". . . justified in defending himself when he apprehended that his life was in danger . . ." At the conclusion of a second trial (the jury on the first trial deadlocked), the jury returned a verdict of not guilty.

THE MAD BOMBER OF BATH

Bath
May 18, 1927

As an ultimate punishment for the people of Bath, he planned to kill their children.

Andrew Kehoe, a distinguished-looking, 47-year-old farmer, and his wife Nellie moved to the small village of Bath in 1919. Nellie's uncle, a Bath farmer, had died, and she and Andrew had purchased the farm from relatives who controlled the estate.

Though a frugal and modern farmer who knew machinery, electricity, and explosives, Kehoe struggled to break even on his small Bath farm. In 1921, the residents of Bath and surrounding communities voted to consolidate all of the one-room schoolhouses in the area and, to accommodate the influx of students, greatly expanded Bath's school building. The special assessment to pay for the new addition hit Kehoe particularly hard, and he could no longer make mortgage payments to his wife's family. Nellie, torn between her ties and obligations to her prominent family and struggling Andrew, suffered from severe headaches and asthma attacks and entered a Lansing hospital.

Kehoe became an outspoken critic of the Bath School Board, which he blamed for the tax increase that caused his problems, and, on July 14, 1924, he defeated an incumbent for a position on that board. For the next two years, Kehoe consistently, relentlessly, and sometimes viciously attacked the board's spending policies and also the superintendent, whom Kehoe viewed as extraneous, incompetent and too powerful. Kehoe, who also sat on the board of directors of a newly created farm bureau, firmly established himself as a prominent figure in the community, and, when the township clerk died in April, 1925, the township board chose him to serve out the remaining one year at the position.

But, starting in early 1926, a series of unexpected, humiliating defeats and setbacks all but destroyed Kehoe's power, dignity, and self-image. In April, his own political party snubbed him by not even nominating him for reelection as township clerk. By summer, even Kehoe's most ardent supporters began to express their displeasure with his incessant, often petty, rantings against the school board and efficient superintendent. In October, Nellie's family began foreclosure proceedings on the farm, and Nellie became a virtual invalid, spending most of her time away from Andrew, either in the hospital or in her sisters' care in Lansing. And, as a final humiliation, on April 6, 1927, Kehoe decisively lost in his bid to be elected justice of the peace.

With that defeat, Kehoe turned his anger, guilt, loneliness, and self-hatred into a hideous and deliberate plan of murderous revenge on Nellie, her family, the school board, the superintendent, and the people of the town of Bath. To take revenge on Nellie for leaving him and siding with her family he would kill her; to financially injure her family he would demolish their new school and kill their superintendent. And, as the ultimate horror of his plan, to punish the people of Bath, he would kill their children.

Without changing the outward appearance of his daily routine, Kehoe spent nearly a month carefully preparing for his final nightmarish acts of revenge. During the day, Kehoe, who had accumulated nearly a ton of explosives, stayed at the farm and painstakingly placed and wired dynamite and Pyrotol throughout the farmhouse, horse barn, and other outbuildings. After completing that network, Kehoe meticulously placed gasoline cans, rigged with spark plugs, in the same buildings and attached both the explosive and the incendiary system to a switch wired to the house's electrical circuit. After supper each evening, he faithfully visited Nellie at a Lansing hospital and returned home just before dark.

Then, each night after dark, Kehoe drove his year-old Ford pickup truck to the school and secretly unloaded and hid precisely the amount of explosives he knew he could place under the school's foundation in a given evening. After unloading, he drove back to the farm and returned on foot. Working by flashlight in the three-foot crawl space under the school's new addition, Kehoe methodically stapled a main wire every three feet along the main supporting timber that ran under the building's center. To this main wire, he spliced twelve branch circuits which ran to explosive charges placed behind supporting pillars.

On May 8, Kehoe completed his work under the new addition and turned to the more difficult task of setting explosives between the basement ceiling and sub-flooring of the first floor of the old building. To gently push the fragile soldered connections and explosives over the rough divisions and gaps, Kehoe connected several pieces of eavestrough together, placed them in the narrow gaps, and pushed charges of dynamite and wire through the smooth conduit with bamboo poles. By May 10, Kehoe had finished placing his deadly circuit and needed only to place and set a timing device.

Before he connected the timer, Kehoe, on May 16, brought his recuperating wife from Lansing to the farm and killed her. Then, late the next night ater a PTA meeting had finished at the school, Kehoe entered the building and made his way through a familiar trapdoor into the crawl space under the new addition. At the detonator switch he had placed under the school's main entrance, Kehoe connected two batteries and a manual alarm clock. Kehoe set the timing device for 9:45 and returned to the farm.

The light rain that had fallen during the night didn't dampen Andrew Kehoe's spirits as he rose early May 18, 1927, for his long-awaited day of revenge. Shortly before dawn, he wheeled an empty hog chute to the farmhouse door, loaded Nellie's body into it, and pushed it into one of the outbuildings. As Kehoe washed, the sun peered through the blue sky, and familiar green buses unloaded students at the school for their last scheduled day of classes before the summer break. As Kehoe put on his finest suit, the older students began their final exams, and the little children listened to wind-up phonographs or stories read by their teachers.

At 9:45 a.m. Kehoe threw a switch that simultaneously exploded and ignited every building on his farm. A split second later, he heard a thundering blast come from town. As black smoke billowed into the air from his farm buildings, Kehoe headed for town in his pickup.

In town, the tremendous force of the blast under the two-story school threw giant chunks of foundation onto the lawn as the accompanying compression forced floors up and walls out. The roof, anchored at the rear by a surviving wall, held for a second or two, then, as the front walls and supports disintegrated, the giant cover shuddered and crushed the first and second floors and occupants in an avalanche of battered wreckage. The rear of the roof leaned precariously against the back wall as, for a few seconds of eerie silence, a haze of white plaster dust settled over everything.

The blast hurled, tossed, and crushed children, teachers, desks, concrete, and wood into a mass of indistinguishable rubble. Buried in the rubble, but still alive, a sixth-grade teacher peered into the darkness and looked directly into the open but lifeless eyes of a small boy crushed and pinned across her broken legs. Outside, the body of a third-grader dangled upside down, like a discarded doll, from the wrecked entranceway. A child's head, covered with thick white plaster dust, protruded from under the roof's edge. Except for a few such visible bodies and parts of bodies, the roof blocked the view of the slaughter.

The roof also obstructed rescue attempts, and buried children screamed and moaned as desperate parents and other rescuers dug with bare hands at the rubble. As men dug furiously, women in housedresses carried injured children to houses across the street. Others carried dead bodies to a grassy knoll in the school yard and placed blankets over them.

At 10:00 a.m., Andrew Kehoe approached the scene and was stunned to see that, because his detonating batteries weren't powerful enough to set off all the explosives, only the north wing and entrance were destroyed. The south wing stood intact, and most of the school's three hundred children, teachers, and superintendent had escaped and were mingling on the grounds with the rescuers and distraught parents. Spotting the superintendent, Kehoe lurched his pickup to a stop and called him over.

As the superintendent stepped off the curb, Kehoe detonated his dynamite-laden truck. A huge ball of smoke shot into the blue sky, and flames shot under a block-long line of rescuers' cars parked in the street. Shrapnel and chunks of flesh blew in all directions, and the upper half of Kehoe's body, head and face undamaged, landed in a garden seventy-five feet diagonally across the street. The superintendent lay dead on the sidewalk, and another man was blown dead against a tree in the school yard. A flying bolt pierced the heart of a young father pulling children from the school wreckage fifty feet away, and an eight-year-old boy, who had escaped the school explosion, died in the truck blast. Flesh and intestines dangled from overhead wires and the steering wheel of Kehoe's truck. As the already stunned parents and rescuers looked unbelievingly at the maimed and dead bodies and wrecked automobiles, a souvenir hunter calmly walked up to Kehoe's truck, snipped a piece of intestine from the steering wheel, and placed it in a jar of alcohol.

With Kehoe's final blast, Michigan's most hideous mass murder finally ended. In all, forty-five persons died, including thirty-eight students and teachers.

BLOODY JULY

Detroit
July 22, 1930

Suddenly, revolvers roared and furniture splintered as the men pumped eleven shots.

When, on July 16, 1920, the 18th amendment to the U.S. Constitution became effective and prohibition became national, illicit liquor operators turned to Canada for supplies. Liquor flowed freely across the Detroit River, and Detroit quickly became the funnel through which millions of gallons of bootlegged booze flowed to the Midwest. Much of the hootch stayed in Detroit, and, by the late twenties, as many as 25,000 illegal saloons and "blind pigs" did $215 million worth of business in the city. And, by 1930, the federal government cited Detroit as leading the nation in prohibition violations.

Criminal gangs controlled bootlegging and other illegal enterprises, and their intense competition for territory left its bloody mark on Detroit. Gang members ruthlessly executed rival hoodlums who encroached on their well-defined turf, and Detroit streets resounded with gunfire and bomb explosions. Detroit's 232 recorded homicides in 1925 included fifty-three gangsters whose bodies were recovered from the Detroit River, thirty-three by dragging and twenty "floaters." But, as Detroit became a veritable shooting gallery, the average citizen was seldom in jeopardy and only read about the gangster murders in newspaper reports.

The quality of the police force and their response to the gangs' activities was dismal. Some policemen themselves were bootleggers. Others routinely drank at blind pigs, slept on their beats, burglarized, or committed armed robberies. Gangs routinely paid policemen, judges, revenue agents, and politicians for protection. When, on the rare occasion the police did arrest a bootlegger, most people believed it was simply because the criminal hadn't paid off.

Many citizens blamed Detroit Mayor Charles Bowles for the lawlessness, unchecked corruption, and loose law enforcement, and, in late spring, 1930, a group called the Citizen's League launched a recall campaign against the mayor. The recall election was scheduled for July 21, 1930.

As the election approached, during the first two weeks of July, gangsters gunned down ten men in the worst outbreak of gangland slaying to that time. An outraged public termed the period "Bloody July," and wondered whether their city was being run by gangsters or government.

Radio commentator Jerry Buckley echoed and championed the citizens' frustration and outrage with the lawless state of their city. Since 1929, thousands of loyal listeners had gathered around their radios to listen to Buckley emotionally attack illegal gambling, gang warfare, corrupt politicians, and other local evils that threatened to overwhelm the powerless "little man." Hundreds of Buckley fan clubs formed throughout the city, and the expose' reporter became a powerful former of public opinion.

On the eve of the recall election, July 20, 1930,

Buckley, who had spoken against the recall, suddenly did a complete about-face, bitterly attacked Bowles and the inept police, and strongly supported the recall movement. On election day, Buckley broadcast voting trends and results from city hall then, shortly after midnight, climaxed his radio fight against Bowles and crime conditions by announcing that the mayor had been recalled.

Buckley then went to the LaSalle Hotel, sat in a lobby chair, and waited for an unknown woman who had called him during his city hall broadcasts. As prostitutes sauntered by the lobby window on their way down brightly lit Woodward Avenue, Buckley unfurled a newspaper that detailed the election results and relaxed. At one a.m., three men strolled across the nearly empty lobby to where Buckley sat alone. Suddenly, revolvers roared and furniture splintered as the men pumped eleven shots into Buckley's head and body. The popular reporter slumped dead onto the floor, his bullet-riddled newspaper by his side.

Buckley's shocked audience mourned him as few had been mourned in Detroit. More than 100,000 people filled the streets for Buckley's funeral, and spokesmen from every segment of the community demanded a manhunt for the killers. Detroit police, however, deliberately or unintentionally bungled the murder investigation from the outset. No broadcast of the shooting ever went over the police radio, and two patrolmen, following a promising lead on their own, were transferred from the case. At the height of the public's emotional demands to find the killers, the police commissioner took a vacation.

A later investigation discounted any connection with the Bowles recall as a motive in Buckley's murder, and the general conclusion was that gangsters had executed the reporter because of his radio attacks or even because of his possible financial involvement with underworld figures. The killers were never caught.

THE COLLINGWOOD MASSACRE

Detroit
September 16, 1931

The three independents had committed the unpardonable underworld sin of conducting their business within the Purple Gang's territory.

Of all the mobs involved in bootlegging and the rackets in Detroit during the prohibition era, the most notorious and vicious was the Purple Gang. Though the gang only numbered about fifty-one members, they effectively warred with other Detroit mobs for underworld supremacy and may have killed as many as five hundred members of their competition during the prohibition era. Purple Gang killers became legendary as the most proficient in the underworld, and Al Capone may have borrowed three to carry out his infamous 1929 St. Valentine's Day Massacre in Chicago.

The Purple Gang's murders reached a bloody climax with the mass killing of three underworld figures on Detroit's northwest side on September 16, 1931. Joseph Sutker, Herman Paul, and Joseph Lebovitz had left the Purple Gang to become "independent" bootleggers but committed the unpardonable underworld sin of trying to conduct their business within the Purple Gang's strictly defined district boundaries. On September 16, four Purple Gang members, including the gang's two leaders, picked up the three independents at their Selden Street "Handbook Agency" and drove them to an "amicable conference" to settle the conflict. At about three p.m., the group arrived at an apartment house on Collingwood Avenue in the heart of a quiet residential neighborhood.

As Sutker, Paul, and Lebovitz lit fresh cigars in the second-story apartment, the four Purples pulled pistols and fired fifteen shots into the men. The four assassins then ran down the stairway to a waiting automobile, pausing only to drop the murder weapons, serial numbers filed off, into a paint can at the bottom of the stairway.

But the paint did not obliterate the killers' fingerprints, and they were caught, tried, and convicted. Over the next two years, twenty-six more Purples ended up in jail, and sixteen died violently as other gangs moved in to take over the leaderless Purples' territory. In 1933, with the end of prohibition and the beginning of the State Liquor Control Commission, the few surviving members of the Purple Gang were quietly absorbed into other underworld groups, and the short, violent life of the Purple Gang ended.

RIOT AT THE ROUGE

Dearborn
March 7, 1932

As firemen sprayed icy cold water on the crowd, two guns flashed through the gate's openings.

During the late 1920s, many people still considered automobiles a luxury rather than a necessity, so, when the Great Depression struck, it quickly ravaged the workers of Michigan's leading industry, automobile production. In 1932, Michigan's unemployment rate rose to 43 percent compared to a national average of 24 percent. State unemployment or relief organizations didn't exist, so children scavenged through streets, like animals, for scraps of food while their fathers sold apples on street corners or stood in bread lines funded by private relief agencies. But by 1932, these overburdened private agencies were on the verge of collapse, and conservative politicians refused to support public relief programs, partly because they feared that unemployed workers were being directed by communists to overthrow existing economic and political structures.

In Detroit, the situation of unemployed auto workers grew desperate, and, on March 7, 1932, three thousand workers marched toward Henry Ford's Dearborn Rouge Assembly Plant to demand relief for laid-off employees, union recognition, and better working conditions. Communists had planned and led the march, but nearly all the participants were unsuspecting workers seeking promises of aid. At the Dearborn city limits, forty policemen refused the crowd entry because the marchers hadn't obtained a parade permit. When the angry marchers tried to go around the police, the officers hurled tear gas and scattered the throng into small groups.

But the people continued to make their way, over open fields and along side streets, toward the Ford plant. Policemen swinging nightsticks chased the protestors who responded by throwing rocks, chunks of concrete, and pieces of rusty metal at the officers. As the crowd pushed down the street toward the plant gates, hand-to-hand fighting broke out.

The Dearborn Fire Department arrived, but by the time they had connected their hoses, the rioters had reached the locked gates of the Rouge Assembly Plant. Suddenly, as firemen sprayed icy water on the mob, two guns flashed through the gate's openings and fired. Police and Ford security guards leveled their guns also and fired hundreds of shots point-blank into the crowd killing four marchers and spectators. As nearly a hundred wounded people lay screaming and writhing on the cold, wet pavement, the rest of the marchers fled and the battle ended.

Four days later, members of Detroit's 2000-member Communist party further exploited the tragedy by joining nearly 15,000 mourners at the funerals of the slain men and making fiery speeches while hoisting huge pictures of Lenin above the coffins.

A PURGE OF BLOOD
Detroit
May 25, 1935, and May 12, 1936

Pick up a nigger and take him out and shoot him.

By the late 1920s, the Ku Klux Klan had all but died in Michigan, but an even stranger secret brotherhood, bonded by dire oaths, guns, midnight meetings, black hoods and robes, group vengeance, and murder, rose from the Klan's remains. Officially called the United Brotherhood of America, but better known as the Black Legion, the ritualistic society opposed Jews, Blacks, Catholics, and anyone perceived as a threat to white, native-born, "100% Americanism." The foot soldiers in the Legion's battle to purge Michigan of these "anti-American" elements were primarily poorly educated, transplanted, unskilled laborers from the South. But the officers and leaders of the brotherhood were educated, Michigan-born white-collar workers, policemen, firemen, and even state and local government officials.

Upon joining the brotherhood, new members knelt in a circle and chanted a long, rambling oath while veteran members, wearing black satin robes and hoods adorned with white skulls and crossbones, held pistols to their heads. At the conclusion of the initiation ceremony, each new member received a bullet with a warning that a matching bullet would execute him if he violated the organization's secrecy. The new member was then assigned to one of many front organizations to await in-

156

structions.

On May 25, 1935, Legion "Colonel" Harvey Davis issued instructions to Dayton Dean, James Roy Lorance, John Bannerman, and Ervin Lee: "Pick up a nigger and take him out and shoot him." The five went to the home of Silas Coleman, with whom they all worked, and told the 47-year-old, black concrete worker that their foreman had instructed them to bring him to the plant site for payment of $18 in back wages. Before going to the plant site, Coleman stopped with his co-workers at a tavern to celebrate his good fortune.

But then, instead of going to the plant, the five drove Coleman to a marshy area near Pinckney and piled out of their cars. As Coleman came around the rear of a parked car, Harvey Davis shot him twice with a .38 caliber revolver. Stunned, but still able to run, Coleman bolted into a field but became caught on a fence. As Coleman struggled furiously to free himself, the Legion members walked up behind him and calmly shot over thirty rounds of pistol fire into his body.

Almost exactly a year later, at a May 12, 1936, meeting of Detroit's Wolverine Republican League, a Legion front organization, "Colonel" Davis again issued orders. The fifty members present angrily discussed an alleged beating Charles Poole, a 22-year-old WPA worker, had administered to his pregnant wife. Someone claimed, erroneously, that Poole had beaten his wife so severely that her unborn baby had died. Colonel Davis reminded Legion members of their duty to protect American womanhood and ordered Poole executed.

Later that evening, Dayton Dean invited Poole, an avid baseball fan, to an important "baseball meeting." Poole readily accepted and entered Dean's car. As they pulled away, a second car joined them and then a third. In an open area in Dearborn Township, the caravan stopped, and several of the occupants stepped out for a drink. Poole stayed inside, but, twenty minutes later, hooded members brought him in front of the group and accused him of beating his spouse and killing their unborn child. "You've got me wrong," pleaded a terrified Poole. "My wife is in the hospital having the baby right now. She's all right."

Suddenly, from a distance of only six feet, two of the hooded members gunned Poole down. Others then took turns shooting him and left his body, riddled with eight bullet holes, on the ground littered with empty shells and crushed cigarette butts.

Upon the discovery of Poole's body, police launched an intensive investigation, gathered evidence, made arrests, and convinced Dayton Dean to confess. Dean implicated not only his co-assassins but also his immediate Legion superiors. Their arrests and subsequent confessions started a chain reaction that eventually exposed the entire Legion and its crimes. The investigation and confessions ultimately revealed that the Legion claimed more than 200,000 Michigan members and had killed, many by flogging, fifty-seven people in Detroit, alone, from 1931 to 1936.

The trial of the murderers of Charles Poole and Silas Coleman lasted until December 5, 1936. Bannerman, Davis, Lee, and Dean received double life sentences for the murder of Coleman, and eight Legion members were convicted of first-degree murder and four for second-degree murder in Poole's death. Following the convictions, black robes appeared in garbage cans and dumps all over Michigan, and, through trials for other Legion activities, the courts completely destroyed the society by 1939.

THE SHARPSHOOTING DENTIST

Midland
September 29, 1937

As the car sped toward a bridge, Hardy sent two .35 caliber copperhead bullets crashing through the rear window.

As a robber, Anthony Chebatoris had no luck at all and always seemed to pick the wrong time to commit a crime. In 1918, at age twenty, he was convicted in Detroit of armed robbery and sentenced to seven and a half years at Jackson. In 1927, he was arrested in Louisville, Kentucky, for a violation of the Dyer Act. The following year he entered the prison at Marquette on a 7½- to 20-year sentence for the armed robbery of a Packard Motor Company paymaster. By the time he and an old prison friend, Jack Gracey, prepared to rob the Chemical State Savings Bank at Midland, 29-year-old Chebatoris had spent over half his life in prison and was wanted in several other states on various charges.

Chebatoris continued his streak of bad luck as, at 11:30 a.m. on September 29, 1937, he and Gracey entered the Chemical State Savings Bank. Chebatoris pressed a shotgun into the bank president's ribs as Gracey ordered customers and tellers to "stick 'em up." But the president instinctively grabbed the gun and it discharged, wounding the banker in the chest. As a cashier rushed to help his wounded boss, Gracey shot the cashier in the thigh. Chebatoris and Gracey, without taking any money, then panicked and rushed out to the street.

Dr. Frank L. Hardy, a dentist who worked in an office over the bank, heard the shooting below, grabbed an automatic rifle, and, as Chebatoris and Gracey jumped into their car, stepped to his open window. Thirteen other Michigan banks had already been robbed that year, and Hardy, an expert marksman, had kept the rifle at his office just in case someone tried to rob the bank below. As the getaway car sped toward a bridge crossing the Tittabawassee River, Hardy sent two bullets crashing through the vehicle's rear window. One struck Chebatoris, the driver, in the arm and he crashed into a parked car. Gracey and Chebatoris jumped out of their wrecked car, and Chebatoris, mistaking a uniformed truck driver for a policeman, shot and killed the innocent bystander. Hardy fired two more shots, and one of the .35 caliber copperhead bullets blew off the back of Gracey's head and flipped him dead on the street. Chebatoris then ran along the nearby railroad tracks but only got about four blocks before police captured him.

If Chebatoris thought his luck couldn't get any worse, he was wrong. Three years earlier, Congress, in an effort to help control a wave of bank robberies and kidnappings, had passed the National Bank Robbery Act.

Under this act, robbing a Federal Reserve or Federal Deposit Insurance Corporation bank became a federal crime. "Bad Luck" Chebatoris had not only committed a federal crime but also, though Michigan had abolished capital punishment for murder in 1846, faced execution since the National Bank Robbery Act also contained a clause that read, "Whoever . . . in . . . attempting to free himself from arrest or confinement for such offense, kills any person . . . shall be punished by . . . death, if the verdict of the jury shall so direct."

At the completion of the Chebatoris trial, the U.S. District Attorney argued for the death penalty, the jury complied, and Anthony Chebatoris was sentenced to be executed. Knowing that Michigan had abolished capital punishment, Illinois and Indiana officials offered the use of their electric chairs. The warden of the Cook County, Illinois, jail wrote, "Our chair is ready for your use at any time. We'll make no charge, of course. Always glad to oblige a neighbor."

But a federal judge ruled that the execution could not be moved from Michigan, and, on July 8, 1938, just as the first streaks of sunrise broke over the wall of the Federal Detention Farm at Milan, Chebatoris walked up the traditional thirteen steps to a crude, rough-pine gallows. Guards placed a black hood over his head, strapped his arms and legs, and slipped a noose around his neck. At 5:08 a.m., Chebatoris plummeted nine feet through the gallows' trapdoor, snapped the rope tight from the railroad tie to which it was fastened, and swayed and twisted slowly. Directly under the trap, a two-foot-deep pit had been dug so the examining physician could check the body without difficulty, and, at 5:21 a.m., the doctor pronounced Chebatoris dead.

"Bad Luck" Chebatoris was the first person tried under the National Bank Robbery Act, the first person executed under the act, and the last person executed in the State of Michigan.

THE WAR
WITHIN MICHIGAN
Detroit
June 20-21, 1943

The crowd dispersed but returned to their neighborhoods with false, outrageous stories.

By the late thirties, Michigan had pulled out of the depths of the Great Depression, and times were gradually improving. Adding to the state's pride and self-respect, Detroit became the "City of Champions" with the Tigers winning the American League pennant in 1934 and 1935, the Lions capturing the National Football League crown in 1935, the Red Wings taking the Stanley Cup in the same year, and the "Brown Bomber," Joe Louis, pounding his way to the World Heavyweight Boxing Championship in 1937.

But during this same period, blacks made painfully slow advances in civil rights and living conditions, and Detroit was a model of racial segregation. Detroit's 150,000 blacks were jammed into segregated ghettoes where they paid exorbitant rents for overcrowded, unsanitary, dilapidated dwellings. Attracted by jobs in the booming auto factories, more blacks streamed into the city until, by the time the Japanese attacked Pearl Harbor, the housing situation for Detroit's black residents had become intolerable. Also flooding into the city and competing for the same jobs were hundreds of thousands of southern whites who brought with them their deep-seated racism. World War II erupted, and black leaders hoped that, as the state pulled together in the war effort, these racist attitudes and policies would diminish.

Michigan's factories quickly and efficiently retooled to produce war materials, and Michigan became the "Arsenal of Democracy," but Detroit remained a closed society for blacks. In February, 1942, two hundred black families tried to enter a new public housing project in a white neighborhood on Detroit's northwest side, but over one thousand whites, coming from as far as twenty-five miles away and armed with clubs, rifles, and knives, forced them to leave. It took three months and a contingent of 2400 Michigan State troops and state police to finally move fourteen families into the project. The following June, 25,000 Packard Motor Car Company workers defied the UAW and walked off their jobs to protest "mixing black and white workers on the same job." Black servicemen bitterly complained that they fought and died in a segregated military merely to preserve their right to remain second-class citizens.

Racial hostility in Detroit finally exploded. On Sunday, June 20, 1943, over 100,000 blacks and whites, seeking relief from the oppressive heat and humidity, jammed into tiny Belle Isle's two square miles. Whites and blacks aggressively competed for the inadequate number of boats, horses, bicycles, picnic spots, and hot dog stands, and, by late afternoon, tempers, as well as the temperature, broiled. At about nine p.m., thousands of hot, tired, and irritable picnickers jammed across the narrow bridge to return to the mainland. As they jostled and shoved through the bottleneck, a fight broke out and then, quickly, several others. Two hundred uniformed white sailors from a nearby armory joined in, and, by the time the police arrived, hundreds of blacks and whites battled in isolated skirmishes. Most of the huge crowd, however, just stood and watched, and, by midnight, the police restored order without firing a shot.

The crowd dispersed but returned to their neighborhoods with false, outrageous stories that incited a riot. A young black man, impersonating a police officer, jumped onto the stage at a dance hall in the heart of a ghetto called Paradise Valley, grabbed the microphone from the orchestra leader, and told the seven hundred persons inside, "There's a riot at Belle Isle. The whites have thrown a colored lady and her baby off the bridge." The club emptied, and blacks first destroyed white-owned stores in the ghetto then vented their fury by stoning passing white motorists and pedestrians. In the meantime, whites had returned to midtown Detroit, inhabited by mostly southern, white factory workers, with the story that blacks had raped and murdered a white woman on the Belle Isle bridge. White gangs quickly formed and surged through downtown Detroit, overturning autos driven by blacks, beating the drivers, and dragging black passengers out of streetcars and beating them also.

By Monday morning, the violence was generating death. Shortly before dawn, blacks beat a white pedestrian and left him unconscious in the street where a taxicab ran over him. Later that morning, Dr. Joseph DeHoratiis, a white physician who had many black patients, disregarded police warnings and entered Paradise Valley on a house call. Minutes after passing the police barricade, a rioter hit Dr. DeHoratiis in the head with a rock then reached inside the doctor's car and beat him to death. Early Monday afternoon, a mob of T-shirted white men and boys beat a black youth to death on the steps of the Federal Building as, inside, officials prepared to request troops.

Though black rioters numbered only in the hundreds and white rioters numbered in the tens of thousands, the nearly all-white police department concentrated its attention on blacks in Paradise Valley and did little to stop rampaging whites. Without police interference, whites chased and beat innocent blacks and piled into cars and fired at blacks with shotguns and rifles as they sped past. Blacks soon saw the police, who ultimately killed seventeen blacks but no whites, not as a neutral force but as part of the white mob.

Finally, by Monday night, the first of five thousand federal troops arrived and rolled through Detroit streets in armored cars and jeeps bristling with automatic weapons. The troops used rifle butts to disperse one last mob of two thousand whites who had gathered on the perimeter of Paradise Valley, and the riot ended.

Thirty-six hours of savagery left nine whites and twenty-five blacks dead and five hundred injured. On August 11, 1943, a governor's committee report placed most of the blame for the riot on Detroit's black community, a report almost universally termed a "whitewash."

SILENCING A SENATOR

Springport
January 11, 1945

The ultimate resolution of this scandal left many questions unanswered.

While the governor's committee was attempting to quickly end the controversy spawned by the Detroit riot, another story began filtering out of Lansing involving charges of legislative bribery and political corruption. Rumors spread throughout the state that special interest groups, through lobbyists, were purchasing the votes of legislators and that large slush funds existed to buy every possible kind of favorable legislation.

In response to the stories, Ingham County Judge Leland Carr was named as a one-man grand jury, and Kim Sigler was appointed as a special prosecutor to investigate. Sigler had no difficulty substantiating the rumors and, within a month, persuaded Judge Carr to indict twenty state legislators and six automobile finance company officials for plotting to corrupt the state legislature.

The investigation continued, and Sigler scheduled two key witnesses, Charles F. Hemans and Warren G. Hooper, to appear before Judge Carr. Hemans, a prominent lobbyist, had unexpectedly turned state's evidence and revealed that he had kept records of payments to legislators from bankers, loan companies, racetrack operators, slot-machine owners and others. Sigler had granted immunity to Hooper, a Republican state senator from Albion, and the lawmaker was scheduled to testify in several cases, including that of former Republican National Committeeman Frank D. McKay, whom Sigler suspected of participating in a horse racing conspiracy.

On January 11, 1945, the day before Hooper was scheduled to first testify, an unknown driver took the senator from Lansing toward Albion and, at about 5:30 p.m., pulled the car off to the side of M-99 about three miles north of Springport. There, the driver shot Hooper in the left cheek, under the left ear, and in the left side of the head with a .38 caliber pistol at such close range that powder burns ringed the three wounds. The killer then opened the driver's side door, set the car and Hooper's body on fire, walked calmly through the snow to another car that had pulled alongside, and disappeared.

Hooper's murder crippled the grand jury investigation. With his star witness dead, Sigler was forced to drop the case against McKay, and, when Hemans suddenly refused to testify and fled the state, the investigation all but ended. The grand jury indicted 125 men, forty-six were convicted, and the political careers of many legislators were ruined. But the ultimate resolution of this scandal — a rare occurrence in Michigan's political history — left many questions unanswered, including the main one — who killed Senator Hooper? Though three Detroit men, reputedly former members of the Purple Gang (see p. 152),were convicted of conspiring to kill the senator, the assassin was never found.

LOOK WHAT I'VE DONE

Byron Center
February 25, 1949

Martha's insane jealousy over Raymond's romantic attentions to his victims caused their cheap con game to go amuck.

Mrs. Deliphine Downing, an attractive, 28-year-old, Byron Center widow, waited anxiously for a visit from the man who she hoped would fill the gap in her life. Two lonely years after the unexpected death of her husband, Mrs. Downing had placed an ad in a magazine's "lonely hearts club," and 35-year-old Raymond Fernandez, a Hawaiian-born Spaniard who said he had worked for the British Intelligence during World War II, had answered. For months, they carried on a correspondence courtship. Fernandez wrote absolutely charming letters and, when he finally proposed marriage, Mrs. Downing eagerly accepted and invited Fernandez and his sister to immediately move in with her.

On January 19, 1949, a slim, elegantly dressed, mustached man and a huge woman walked up the pathway to the Downing house. Mrs. Downing's three-year-old daughter, Rainelle, hid behind her mother's skirt as Fernandez introduced himself. Then, bending down with a friendly smile, Fernandez said, "Hello, Rainelle. Don't be such a shy little girl." His gentle manner coaxed a smile from the little girl and enchanted Mrs. Downing. Fernandez then turned to the five-foot, seven-inch, 200-pound woman standing behind him and introduced her as his sister, Martha. Mrs. Downing quickly reassured Martha that she was welcome since her presence would help prevent scandalous gossip in the neighborhood.

Ray and Martha then moved into Downing's five-room cottage. Fernandez quickly seduced their hostess, took her to Long Island where he married her, then spent the next five weeks advising her to sell all of her property.

On a rainy February 25, after Mrs. Downing had converted almost all of her assets, including her home, to cash, Martha and Ray fed the former widow an overdose of sleeping pills. The pills worked slowly, and Fernandez, seeing Mrs. Downing uncomfortably struggling against their effects, shot her in the head then carried her body to the basement and threw it in a deep pit he had dug.

Little Rainelle, not knowing where her mother had gone, sobbed loudly for two days. To comfort and distract the child, Martha and Raymond bought her a dog, but Rainelle ignored the animal and continued to cry, "Where's my mommy. I want my mommy." Finally Fernandez screamed to Martha, "Can't you do something about her?" Martha nodded, calmly picked up the crying child, threw her into a washtub, and held her under the water until she drowned. Fernandez then carried the tiny, limp body to the cellar, laid it next to Mrs. Downing's body in the pit, filled the hole with cement, and used a hair dryer to help the new concrete set.

But neighbors, suspicious at the sudden disappearance of Rainelle and her mother, notified police, and, during the early morning of March 1, 1949, officers arrived at the house and questioned Fernandez. Fernandez confidently invited them to "search the house if you like." Police accepted his foolish invitation and found in the basement, not concealed at all, a fresh patch of cement the size of a grave. Police dug down four feet and found the bodies of Mrs. Downing and Rainelle.

Knowing that Michigan had no death penalty for murder, Martha and Raymond talked freely, not only about the Downing murders, but also of other victims, as they unraveled a bizarre tale of a love and life financed by a cheap con game and murder. For years, Fernandez had made his living seducing lonely women. He had concentrated on females in their late 50s and early 60s, answered their lonely hearts ads in magazines, swept them off their feet with lavish attention and charm, swindled them out of all their money, then abandoned them. Then, in December, 1947, Fernandez answered an ad from 28-year-old Martha Beck, a Pensacola, Florida, divorced nurse and fell in love with the 200-pound woman. When he admitted his con game to her, Martha enthusiastically approved and offered to help. So, together, they made a business out of Ray's ability to charm and fleece lovelorn women. Fernandez would join a lonely hearts club, charm a vulnerable woman, and introduce the lady to his "sister" Martha.

But Martha's insane jealousy over Fernandez's romantic attentions to his own victims caused their con game to go amuck and turned them into murderers. In less than two years, Beck and Fernandez traveled a path strewn with as many as seventeen grisly killings, including the murder of Janet Fay. Prior to coming to Byron Center, Beck and Fernandez had moved into Janet Fay's New York apartment and had obtained every penny of the 66-year-old widow's savings. As they prepared to leave, Mrs. Fay cried out for her beloved Fernandez, and Martha, in a jealous rage, crushed the woman's skull with a hammer. As Janet Fay quivered on the floor, Martha turned to Ray and, in mock horror, giggled, "Look what I've done." Ray then strangled the moaning victim with a scarf. After cleaning up the flat to stop blood from dripping through to the apartment below, Beck and Fernandez made passionate love on the floor next to the body. The pair then stuffed Fay's body into a trunk, took it to a small house some miles from New York City, neatly wrapped it in brown butcher paper, and buried it beneath four feet of concrete. Fernandez, still expecting a Michigan trial and a life sentence with possible parole in sixteen years, generously gave Byron Center police the address of the cottage.

By March 2, the day after the discovery of the Downing bodies, Beck and Fernandez had been charged with the murders of Deliphine Downing, Rainelle Downing, and Janet Fay. But, to the pair's shock, Michigan authorities extradited them to New York where they were tried for the murder of Janet Fay, found guilty, and sentenced to death. On March 8, 1951, Raymond Fernandez was electrocuted in New York's Sing Sing prison electric chair. Martha Beck followed him twelve minutes later.

ANATOMY OF A MURDER

Big Bay
August, 1952

The Mather Inn in Ishpeming has dedicated its lobby
to a celebrated rape and murder that took place at nearby Big Bay in 1952. Actually, the rape and murder were
not celebrated until J.D. Voelker, former Marquette
County prosecutor and Michigan Supreme Court justice,
used the crimes as the basis of a best selling, largely
autobiographical novel published, in 1958, with the title,
Anatomy of a Murder.

Writing under the pseudonym, Robert Traver,
Voelker quickly provides graphic details of the thinly fic-
tionalized rape and murder. On a beautiful August
night, voluptuous Laura Manion, face and arms badly
bruised, skirt torn, and panties missing, staggers up to
the trailer she shares with her army husband. Through
bruised and bleeding lips, she sobs that hotel and bar
owner Barney Quill has raped and beaten her. After
cleaning and comforting his wife, Lieutenant Frederick
Manion, heavily decorated veteran of World War II and
Korea, stuffs a Luger into his pocket and drives the half
mile to Quill's Thunder Bay Inn. Manion calmly enters
the inn, walks to the bar, and, without uttering a sound,
shoots Quill. As Quill slumps to the floor, Manion con-
tinues to rip shots into the rapist's body until the Luger
empties and clicks several times. Manion then drives back
to the trailer park and tells the caretaker to call the state
police.

172

Forty-year-old Paul Biegler, local lawyer and former prosecutor for "Iron Cliffs" (Marquette) County, decides to defend Manion, and Voelker dramatically reconstructs the investigation and trial through Biegler's folksy words and wry sense of humor. Biegler's job, as he sees it, is to admit the murder, arouse sympathy for beautiful, but promiscuous, Laura, and build his defense on the somewhat tenuous psychiatric foundation termed "irresistible impulse."

But Biegler's job is complicated from the outset. He dislikes Lieutenant Manion, an arrogant egotist with a nasty jealous streak and a tendency to attack any man who admires his wife. The prosecuting attorney, who happens to be Biegler's opponent in an upcoming congressional election, brings in a crack assistant from the state attorney general's office in Lansing. All Biegler has are his own wits and experience and the assistance of an attractive secretary and an able, but often drunk, colleague.

But Biegler scrounges for evidence and plans his defense strategy so well that there is never any serious doubt about the verdict that ends *Anatomy of a Murder*.

In 1959, the movie, *Anatomy of a Murder*, was filmed on location, and the lobby of Ishpeming's Mather Inn contains a gallery of autographed pictures of the celebrities — Otto Preminger, James Stewart, George C. Scott, Lee Remick, Ben Gazzara, and Duke Ellington — who stayed there during the filming.

KILLED IN THE FREE STORE

Detroit
July 23 - 30, 1967

Blacks and whites loaded cars and trucks with groceries, furniture, cigarettes, and every other conceivable type of merchandise.

At 3:45 a.m., on a hot and humid Sunday, July 23, 1967, twelve Detroit policemen prepared to make another routine raid on an illegal, after-hours drinking establishment in the dilapidated, predominantly black 12th Street area. At 4:00 a.m., officers smashed the "blind pig's" door with a sledgehammer and arrested the bartender and eighty-two customers.

As paddy wagons arrived to remove the arrested persons, hundreds of spectators gathered and began to taunt and insult the police. An hour and four paddy wagon trips later, the last police car pulled away. As it did, an empty liquor bottle shot from the crowd, arched through the air, and crashed through the car's rear window. The crowd cheered then broke up into smaller groups which moved slowly and noisily down 12th Street. Suddenly, a litter basket was thrown through a store window, and hands reached inside and yanked out merchandise. More glass shattered and a riot that reached a scale unknown in the 20th Century began.

Police returned quickly to the area but, vastly outnumbered, stood helplessly by while the growing mob looted stores. Despite an undercurrent of tension, a

174

carnival-like atmosphere prevailed, and the mob cheerfully smashed windows and ransacked stores until, by mid-morning, six blocks of 12th Street was in shambles.

Before noon, respected black community leaders arrived, and, when they tried to calm the rioters and urged them to return home, they were pelted with rocks, bricks, and verbal abuse.

Still outnumbered, police refrained from forceful action against looters, and, as the mob grew larger and bolder, the west side of Detroit became a free store. Both blacks and whites, sometimes helping each other, loaded cars and trucks with groceries, furniture, cigarettes, and every other conceivable type of merchandise. Some motorists drove home with couches tied across car roofs and rugs on the fenders.

By noon, arsonists had set fires, and, when firemen arrived, the rioters pelted them with bottles, rocks, and bricks. In most cases, firemen were forced to stand helplessly at a distance while buildings burned.

As conditions grew worse, Governor Romney, at the request of Detroit Mayor Jerome Cavanaugh, proclaimed a state of emergency and ordered the State Police and National Guard to assist Detroit police. At three p.m., as State Police arrived, looting and arson spilled out of the 12th Street area and spread to other main streets on both Detroit's East and West sides. By 7:00 p.m., the first National Guardsmen were on the streets. Neither by experience, temperament, nor training were the guardsmen prepared to cope with such a situation. As a result, both officers and men often panicked, and the Guard was involved in eleven riot deaths, including nine innocent victims. Police, also, were no longer restraining themselves and often shot looters on sight.

By midnight Sunday, five thousand people on the West Side and three thousand on the East Side were involved in looting and destruction, and Mayor Cavanaugh and Governor Romney recognized that additional help was needed. At three a.m. Monday morning, July 24, Romney phoned U.S. Attorney General Ramsey Clark and requested five thousand federal troops.

For the next twenty-four hours, Romney and members of President Lyndon B. Johnson's staff, concerned about the political ramifications of their actions, argued over legal technicalities and semantics of the request for troops, and the riot raged on. Looters danced in the eerie shadows, stripping stores then setting them on fire. By 6:00 a.m. Monday, fires raged out of control, and whole sections of the nation's fifth largest city lay in charred smoking ruins. National Guard armored personnel carriers and tanks mounted with .50 caliber machine guns rolled through the smoke-filled streets. The National Guardsmen's fear turned to hysteria as grossly exaggerated reports of sniper fire poured into police headquarters. For the next two days, the tense and apprehensive Guard sent a barrage of bullets into the riot area.

By dawn Tuesday, July 25, federal paratroopers finally arrived, and a state of war existed in Detroit as the regular army troops, armed with M-16 rifles, M-79 grenade launchers, and tear gas, deployed on the East Side. Two days later, the commander of the federal troops had finally successfully established control over both the unrestrained guardsmen and rioters. By the time federal troops left the city on July 30, 3,800 people had been arrested, 1,700 stores had been looted, 1,383 buildings had been burned, and 347 people had been injured. Forty-three persons died in the riot. The victims who lost their lives:

KRIKOR MESSERLIAN, 67 (July 23, 2:30 p.m.) — As a gang of black youths attempted to break into the store next to Messerlian's shoe repair shop, the small Armenian immigrant swung a twenty-inch sabre, an old momento, at them. One of the youths returned soon after and clubbed the shop owner to death, making him the riot's first fatality.

WILLIAM HUNTER and PRINCE WILLIAMS (July 23) — The two young black men entered a drugstore in an area of heavy looting and disappeared when the building caught fire. Three days later, their bodies were found in the burned rubble of the store.

SHEREN GEORGE, 23 (July 23, 11:30 p.m.) — After giving two friends a ride to the fringes of the riot area, Sheren, her husband, and two other friends headed home. Suddenly, a pistol shot shattered through the left rear door of their car and ripped into the pregnant woman's left side below her breast. Sheren, whose first husband had been shot to death several years before, died two hours later.

WALTER GRZANKA, 45 (July 24, 12:05 a.m.) — As the son of Polish immigrants helped a group of blacks loot a grocery store, the owner drove up and fired at the group with a .22 revolver. Grzanka fell to the sidewalk with a bullet hole in his left chest, just above his coat pocket which held seven cigars, four packages of pipe tobacco, and nine pair of shoelaces from the market. Grzanka died twenty-five minutes later.

JULIUS DORSEY, 55 (July 24) — The newly hired, black private security guard defended a market from three would-be looters by firing pistol shots into the air. Drawn by the sounds of gunfire, a police patrol car carrying three National Guardsmen sped to the scene. As the would-be looters fled, the Guardsmen opened fire, killing one person — Julius Dorsey.

CLIFTON PRYOR (July 24) — Pryor and six other men, carrying blankets and buckets of water, went to the roof of their apartment house to extinguish sparks flying from nearby burning buildings. A National Guardsman, mistaking Pryor for a sniper, shot and killed the father of four.

JOHN ASHBY, 24 (July 24, 3:30 a.m.) — While fighting a blaze set by an arsonist at a supermarket, the young fireman climbed an aerial ladder and brushed a 4,800-volt wire. Ashby died August 5, 1967, from the effects of the electric shock.

HERMAN ECTOR, 30 (July 24) — A private security guard shot Ector, a black army veteran, with a rifle when Ector protested the guard's rough treatment of suspected looters.

FRED WILLIAMS, 49 (July 24) — A falling high tension wire, dislodged by spreading fires, electrocuted the black laborer as he frantically carried his possessions out of his burning home.

DANIEL JENNINGS, 36 (July 24) — Jennings and two friends smashed the glass of a liquor store door. As Jennings entered, the white owner shot and killed him with a rifle.

ROBERT BEAL, 49 (July 24) — The black auto worker and his brother-in-law drove from their East Side neighborhood to view the riot-torn West Side. As Beal stood in front of an auto parts store that was being looted, a policeman fired a shotgun blast which struck and killed him.

JOSEPH CHANDLER (July 24) — Police fired at

Chandler as he scaled a fence and fled after looting a store near his residence. Hours later, the Korean War veteran died under a car where he had hidden after being shot.

HERMAN CANTY, 46 (July 24) — Canty backed his pickup truck next to a grocery store, filled the vehicle with several boxes of food, then threw a fire bomb into the store. As he sped away police killed the auto worker in a hail of gunfire.

ALFRED PEACHLUM (July 24, 4:00 p.m.) — Peachlum and another man were rummaging through a grocery store when police officers entered and ordered them to halt. The two men ran, and, as they reached the rear door, Peachlum, a black welder, turned toward the police. Spotting something shiny in Peachlum's hand, the police opened fire with shotguns. Peachlum fell dead to the floor, his hand still clutching a piece of meat wrapped in a shiny foil wrapper.

ALPHONSO SMITH, 35 (July 24) — The black waiter and four other men stepped into a store that had been looted bare the day before. Police apprehended the five, and one of the officers, according to the police report, slipped on some debris and accidentally discharged his gun into Smith's neck killing him.

NATHANIEL EDWARDS, 23 (July 24, 4:30 p.m.) — A white man stepped up to Edwards, a black welder and veteran who was visiting his aunt near the riot area, and, for no apparent reason, shot and killed him with a shotgun.

CHARLES KEMP (July 24, 5:00 p.m.) — Police and National Guardsmen shot the black construction laborer in the back as he ran down an alley after stealing five packs of cigars.

RICHARD SIMS (July 24, 8:30 p.m.) — Police shot the unarmed black auto worker as he fled after unsuccessfully trying to break into the back door of a bar.

FRANK TANNER, 19 (July 24, 9:30 p.m.) — Police and guardsmen shot the black looter as he ran from a liquor store. Tanner staggered about a block before dying in the grass of an apartment building yard where his body remained for nearly eleven hours.

CARL SMITH (July 24, 11:30 p.m.) — The fireman hid behind a trash receptacle as police and guardsmen exchanged gunfire with snipers. When Smith raised his head to look around, a stray, .30 caliber bullet cracked into his forehead, and he pitched forward onto the pavement dead.

HENRY DENSON, 27 (July 25, 12:05 a.m.) — As Denson and two friends drove to his apartment, they stopped for a traffic light near a National Guard checkpoint. The light turned green, the driver drove forward, and a voice hollered, "Halt!" As the driver stepped on the brake, a shot rang out, and Denson, sitting in the front passenger's seat, slumped dead after a Guardsman's bullet tore through his right shoulder and out through his neck.

MANUAL COSBEY, 27 (July 25, 12:17 a.m.) — Police shot the black hospital worker as he fled from a store with loot in his hands.

RONALD EVANS, 24, and WILLIAM JONES, 25 (July 25) — Four black men, including Evans and Jones, broke into a neighborhood grocery store and began looting it. Police arrived, surrounded the store, and, after entering it, shot and killed Jones. Police then made Evans lie down on the sidewalk outside and, when Evans suddenly jumped up and ran, also shot and killed him.

JEROME OLSHOVE, 32 (July 25, 3:00 a.m.) — As the eight-year veteran of the Detroit Police Department tried to arrest a looter, the looter grabbed the officer's shotgun. During a brief struggle, the shotgun went off, blasting Olshove in the stomach. Olshove, whose policeman father was injured in the 1943 riot(see p. 162), was the only policeman killed during the 1967 riot.

ROY BANKS, 46 (July 25, 4:15 a.m.) — Although the riot had spread to his East Side neighborhood, Banks walked toward a bus stop, as usual, to go to work. Patrolling guardsmen, approaching on the street from behind, yelled at Banks to stop, and, when he kept going and didn't answer, the guardsmen blasted a volley of shots which killed the black deaf mute.

ARTHUR JOHNSON, 46, and PERRY WILLIAMS, 43 (July 25) — The two black friends stood talking in front of the empty shell of a pawn shop that had been looted and burned two days before. A police car suddenly screeched around the corner, and, as it raced down the street toward them, the two men dived inside the store. The police, without stopping the car, sprayed the building with bullets and kept on going. "You can come out now," onlookers shouted inside to Johnson and Williams, but no one came out.

JACK SYDNOR, 38 (July 25, 9:15 p.m.) — The drunk black man fired a pistol shot into an alley outside his apartment window then sat calmly, gun in hand, while police forced open the apartment door. Sydnor shot the first policeman to enter who, in return, emptied his gun at Sydnor. Police within the building and on the street then poured a hail of gunfire into the apartment. When the shooting stopped, Sydnor's bullet-ridden body lay dead outside his apartment window.

TONIA BLANDING, 4 (July 25) — A machine gunner on a tank, startled by several gunshots, asked where the shots came from. As the assistant gunner pointed to a nearby apartment house, a flash appeared in a window, and the machine gunner opened fire. Inside the building, one of the .50 caliber bullets struck the little black girl in the chest killing her instantly. Seconds earlier, her uncle, William Hood, while standing in the window, had lit a cigarette.

JOHN LEROY (July 26) — Leroy and four other men headed in a white station wagon to one of the men's homes. As they turned onto the man's street, they found it blocked by a National Guard jeep. Suddenly, for no apparent reason, National Guardsmen, who had hidden behind trees and houses, released a volley of shots which ripped into the car killing Leroy and seriously wounding the others.

AUBREY POLLARD, 19, FRED TEMPLE, 18, and CARL COOPER, 17 (July 26, 12:45 a.m.) — The three black men were partying with two white women at the Algiers Motel, located in the middle of the riot area, when ten policemen and guardsmen stormed in looking for snipers. Pollard, Temple, and Cooper, all unarmed, were shotgunned from a distance of less than fifteen feet, each more than once, and two while lying or kneeling. Two Detroit policemen were later charged with murder but acquitted.

HELEN HALL, 50 (July 26, 1:00 a.m.) — The white, out-of-town businesswoman, while staying at the plush Harlan Hotel, heard tanks rumbling down the streets outside her room. As she threw open her curtains to watch, a rifle slug slammed through the window and into her chest killing her almost instantly.

LARRY POST, 26 (July 26, 2:20 a.m.) — Post's National Guard unit opened fire on a car driven by three black men which had run a blockade. In the ensuing cross fire a slug tore into Post's body, and the bachelor died several weeks later.

GEORGE TALBERT, 20 (July 26) — Talbert and a friend walked into the riot area to survey the damage. As Talbert and his friend, both unarmed, not looting, nor breaking curfew, turned onto a street leading to the riot area, a National Guardsman standing at the end of the street raised his rifle, took careful aim, and fired. The bullet passed through Talbert and also struck his friend. Talbert, a black, laid-off construction worker, died ten days later.

WILLIE McDANIELS (July 26) — After staying in his apartment for the first three days of the rioting, McDaniels went for a walk to look at the riot damage in his neighborhood. As he passed a group of looters coming out of a department store, a police car arrived and shooting broke out. When the gunfire ended, McDaniels lay dead in the street, a bullet hole in his right temple.

JULIUS LUST, 26 (July 26, 9:00 p.m.) — The young black man entered a junkyard to take a part he needed to repair his car. Police, in a car, pulled in front of the gate and ordered him to halt. As Lust turned to run, he raised his hand which held a wrench, and the police, thinking it was a gun, opened fire killing him.

ALBERT ROBINSON, 35 (July 26) — As National Guardsmen stormed into Robinson's apartment building in pursuit of a sniper, the black auto worker stepped into the hallway to take out some trash. According to the Guard's report, Robinson tried to grab one of their men's rifles, so they bayoneted and shot him to death.

WILLIAM DALTON, 19 (July 27, 9:30 p.m.) —
Restless after being shut in for four days because of the
rioting, Dalton walked to visit some friends who lived in
the riot area. Police stopped Dalton, accused him of being an arsonist and a looter, and ordered him to run.
When Dalton refused, the policemen marched him into
an alley and shoved him against the wall. One of the
policemen, standing less than ten feet away, then pointed
a shotgun at Dalton, blasted him in the chest and
stomach, then left.

ERNEST ROQUEMORE, 19 (July 29) — As police
raided Roquemore's apartment building in search of riot
loot, a federal paratrooper with a rifle stationed himself
near the backstairs. Suddenly, a man with something in
his hand that looked like a gun rushed by and the trooper
cocked his rifle. As unarmed Roquemore rushed down
the stairs immediately behind the first man, the trooper
squeezed the trigger and killed the riot's last victim.

THE COED KILLER

Ann Arbor - Ypsilanti
August, 1967 - June, 1969

After the murder of a seventh victim, police finally had a lead.

On August 7, 1967, the mutilated, battered remains of a nineteen-year-old Eastern Michigan University student, who had disappeared a month earlier, were found on a rubbish dump near Ypsilanti. The gruesome discovery was only the first of what would become seven macabre, grisly "coed murders" in the area in the next two years.

The next five victims included:

July 5, 1968 — A twenty-year-old Eastern Michigan University coed whose slashed body was kept in a cellar for several days before being dumped in a field.

March, 1969 — A 23-year-old University of Michigan law student who was shot twice in the head and left on a grave.

March, 1969 — A sixteen-year-old high school dropout and frequent runaway who was sexually abused, whipped, and slashed before being killed by a blow to the head.

April, 1969 — A thirteen-year-old junior high school girl who was garroted with an electric cord, slashed and stabbed in the basement of a farmhouse and her body dumped on a road two-and-a-half miles away.

June, 1969 — A 21-year-old University of Michigan coed who was raped, slashed, and shot in the head and her body dumped in a field.

Through these six brutal slayings, police had no clues

and couldn't determine if the killings were connected or even how many killers were involved.

But, after the murder of a seventh victim, eighteen-year-old Karen Sue Beckemann, police finally had a lead. Several witnesses had seen Karen Sue with a 22-year-old Eastern Michigan University student and motorcycle enthusiast named John Norman Collins. When police further investigated, several of Collins' acquaintances reported that he had hinted he was the coed killer. Police apprehended Collins but, like so many other suspects before, had to release him for lack of any firm evidence.

Soon after, police got the evidence they needed. Mr. and Mrs. Dana Loucks returned to their Ypsilanti home after letting their nephew Collins use it while they were on vacation. Mrs. Loucks discovered a red stain on the floor of their basement and pointed it out to her husband, an Ypsilanti policeman. The stains were quickly proved to be blood of the same type as Karen Sue Beckemann's. Police also determined that hair clippings on the Loucks' basement floor from their two sons' home haircuts matched those found on Karen Sue's underwear.

Based on the hair clippings, the bloodstains, and Collins' admission that he used the Loucks' basement while they were gone, he was convicted and given a life sentence. Collins, who is serving a life sentence at Southern Michigan Prison, has yet to confess to the murder of Karen Sue Beckemann, let alone any of the other six. Though police claimed to have evidence that tied Collins to the other six killings, the murders remain officially unsolved.

MURDER CITY, U.S.A.
Detroit
1973-1974

Mathis was shot to death by a man who didn't like the smell of his feet.

In 1973 and 1974, Detroit became unofficially known as the nation's murder capital. After the 1967 riots, Detroiters armed themselves in record numbers and, by 1974, murdered their fellow citizens at the rate of more than two each day of the year.

From 1967 to 1973, the number of registered guns in the city tripled, and, counting the even greater number of unregistered firearms, an estimated one out of three Detroiters carried guns and didn't hesitate to use them. In early April, 1973, for example, a lawyer at Detroit's Hall of Justice inexplicably drew a gun and pointed it at the judge and a witness. The judge, who usually packed a .38 pistol of his own beneath his robes, didn't have his weapon that day, so three policemen in the courtroom drew their revolvers and shot the lawyer dead. A year later, police killed a sniper during a gun battle in front of police headquarters. Later that same month, Charlie Mathis took off his shoes and was shot to death by a friend who didn't like the smell of Mathis' feet. The murder went down on the police records as a fatal shooting prompted by allegedly "odiferous feet."

Homicide by firearms increased eightfold from 1967 to 1973 as Detroit's nation-leading homicide rate soared to

44.5 murders per 100,000 citizens. Homicide became the fourth leading cause of death in Detroit while in the rest of the nation it was only the eleventh leading killer. Detroit spun in a violent circle — fear of murder prompted more people to buy guns which resulted in even more murders. In 1973, 751 Detroiters, 605 of them black, died at the hands of their fellow citizens. In 1974, the number jumped to an unprecedented 801, and a Massachusetts Institute of Technology study that year claimed that Detroit was the most dangerous city in America in which to be born. A small number, 10 to 12 percent, of murders resulted from executions in underworld battles over narcotics trade. Other victims died during armed robberies and other crimes.

But, in more than half the murders, victim and murderer knew each other or were related, and murder often ended an otherwise routine argument. A 45-year-old black man, for example, arrived home drunk, and, when his wife complained about his drinking, he threatened her with a pistol. She grabbed a shotgun and killed him. Another man shot his girlfriend to death after she refused to give him money from her welfare check. A tenant shot and killed his landlord who asked for rent.

The chances of getting murdered in Detroit became so great that authorities warned against arguing with anyone, especially strangers. In late August, 1974, 64-year-old Joe Peoples ignored the warning and tried to stop a man from stabbing a mongrel dog on an inner-city sidewalk. An hour later, Peoples died of a knife wound in the back.

In 1975, the homicide rate in Detroit declined, for the first time in thirteen years, and Detroit lost its dubious claim to the title of America's murder capital.

THE BLACK LINDBERGH CASE

Detroit
December 1, 1973

The families anxiously sat next to their silent phones waiting for another ransom demand, but the kidnappers had decided on another course of action.

On December 1, 1973, as Detroit's yearly homicide total raced toward a record-breaking 751, six-year-old Keith Arnold played in front of his baby sitter's house, not too far from his own home on Detroit's northwest side. Eight-year-old Gerald Kraft, anonymously well-known to many Americans as a grinning, finger-licking lad who gobbled down Kentucky Fried Chicken on a television commercial, played in his grandmother's yard nearby. During the early evening, Gerald joined Keith, and the two black youngsters played football.

Shortly after six p.m., the boys suddenly disappeared from the street. Two young black men had abducted the unsuspecting children and rushed them to a third man and a young woman waiting at an apartment about five miles away.

Two hours later, a friend of Keith Arnold's mother received a phone call, and a male voice hoarsely whispered a ransom demand of $53,000. Four more times, at 9:50, 10:20, and 11:10 p.m., the caller made the same demand of the Arnold family friend. In the meantime, Mrs. Arnold also received calls warning her not to notify the police if she wanted to see Keith alive again. Gerald Kraft's family, on the other hand, received no phone calls or ransom demands. The kidnappers had picked up Gerald simply because he happened to be playing with Keith and might be able to identify them. Knowing that she could never raise the ransom money, Mrs. Arnold, a divorcee living on a small social security pension from her ex-husband, notified police early the next morning.

That night, the police laid a trap for the kidnappers. The police, through the Arnolds, arranged for a "drop" of ransom money at 8:30 p.m. and prepared a red canvas bag filled with rolled-up newspapers which they brought to the heavily staked out "drop" site. But, at the last moment, the kidnappers ordered the drop spot switched. The police, caught by surprise, could not switch their surveillance detail in time, and the kidnappers got away. For the next thirty-six hours, the families and police anxiously sat next to their silent phones waiting futilely for more ransom demands or threats.

But none would come, for the kidnappers had decided on another course of action. The kidnappers, knowing that a ransom could not be raised, that police were involved, and that Gerald and Keith could identify them, took the two boys from the apartment and drove twenty miles to Romulus. At 7:30 p.m. Monday evening, forty-eight hours after the kidnapping, the men took eight-year-old Gerald and six-year-old Keith into a plowed field about thirty feet from a gravel road near Metro Airport and shot them several times in the head with a .32 caliber pistol.

In the midst of their reign as the nation's "murder

capital," Detroiters had become accustomed, if not actually hardened, to the "routine" daily accounts of homicides, but this new horror temporarily changed that attitude to outrage. "An evil, twisted, and vicious act," said mayor-elect Coleman Young. "A tragedy nearly without parallel in our community," said Police Commissioner Philip Tanian, who ordered more than sixty detectives to work around the clock investigating leads. "A slaughter of innocents," reported the *Detroit News* which posted a $5,000 reward for information leading to the capture of the killers and set up a "secret witness" phone number for informers.

Based on information received through that *News* number, police, on December 5, arrested a nineteen-year-old girl and three 21-year-old men — Byron Smith, Geary Gilmore, and Jerome Holloway — and charged them with first-degree murder. Based on evidence provided by the girl, Smith, Gilmore, and Holloway were convicted and received life sentences.

HEALING AND HOMICIDE

Ann Arbor
July - August, 1975

Hospital security was so lax, just about anyone could have administered the powerful muscle relaxant.

Fox six weeks during July and August, 1975, a mysterious epidemic of breathing failures swept through the Michigan Veterans Administration Hospital in Ann Arbor. Fifty-two patients suffered identical symptoms — a sensation of hands suddenly gripping their lungs and relentlessly squeezing — that left them unable to breathe without mechanical aid. Most of the breathing failures occurred during the afternoon shift in the intensive care unit. Some patients were stricken more than once, and twelve died.

The inordinate number of the quick and unexpected attacks caused patients and staff alike to wonder if a psychopathic doctor or misguided mercy killer ran loose in the hospital. An investigation confirmed their fears: someone had injected Pavulon — a synthetic version of Curare, the lethal plant toxin used by South American Indians to tip their poison darts — into the intravenous feeding tubes of the victims.

The FBI narrowed the list of suspects to two nurses, Leonara Perez, 31, and Filipina Narciso, 29, Phillipine citizens who had lived and worked in the U.S. for six years. The nurses had no previous criminal or anti-social record but had been on duty when and where most of the trouble occurred. On June 16, 1976, a grand jury indicted them on five counts of murder and ten counts of poisoning, but, by the time their case came to trial nine months later, the prosecuting attorney had dropped three of the murder charges and two of the poisoning charges.

The trial started and the government took nine weeks to present its case which consisted entirely of circumstantial evidence. After the testimony of seventy-eight witnesses, the presentation of forty exhibits including the frozen organs of the dead victims, and the introduction of thousands of pages of medical records, the prosecution rested its case without establishing a motive or producing any witnesses that had seen the nurses inject Pavulon into any of the victims' intravenous tubes.

On June 8, 1976, the defense opened its case by submitting a motion to dismiss all charges for lack of evidence. The presiding judge did directly acquit Perez of two murders and four poisonings and Narciso of one murder and three poisonings. But Perez still faced charges for four poisonings and Narciso a murder and five poisonings. Defense attorneys then called a patient who testified that a man wearing green patients' pajamas had entered his room and tampered with his roommate's intravenous tubes then fled shortly before the roommate suffered a respiratory arrest and died. Other testimony implicated a nursing supervisor who had suffered a mental breakdown and committed suicide before the trial. In fact, concluded the defense attorneys, hospital security was so lax, just about anyone could have administered the powerful muscle relaxant to the victims.

On July 13, after deliberating for ninety-four hours, the jury of nine women and three men convicted both Perez and Narciso of three poisonings and acquitted them of all other charges. The convictions triggered demonstrations and protests by nurses, women's groups, and the Phillipine government. Eight hundred people, including uniformed nurses, pajama-clad patients, and six Ypsilanti city councilmen, paraded around the VA hospital grounds claiming that Perez and Narciso had been framed.

The trial judge, in effect, agreed and, on December 19, 1977, overruled the jury's verdict and ordered a new trial. In a 58-page opinion, the judge accused the federal prosecutors of flagrant, unforgiveable conduct and concluded that he was "left with the abiding conviction that this jury's verdicts could not reasonably have been reached free of the influence of the numerous improprieties that occurred during the course of this long trial."

On February 1, 1978, more than a year and a half after the original barrage of indictments against Perez and Narciso, the U.S. attorney in Michigan decided not to retry their case and dropped all remaining charges. No charges were ever filed against anyone else, nor were there any further unusual breathing failures.

THE STRANGE TRAIL

South Haven
January 9, 1976

The report from the FBI came back with a flabbergasting message.

At 9:30 a.m. on October 9, 1971, 32-year-old parolee Richard F. Dixon nervously moved in line with ninety-eight other passengers as they boarded their flight to Miami from Detroit's Metro Airport. Thirty-three passengers and the crew of six had already boarded the Eastern Airlines 727 as Dixon approached the boarding ramp. Suddenly, the St. Clair man whipped out a pistol, cocked it, and held it to the boarding agent's head as he backed into the plane and ordered the door closed.

Dixon then ordered the pilot to fly to Cuba, and, for the next three hours, sat calmly in the passenger section with his pistol pointed at the head of the stewardess who sat next to him. The plane landed without incident, Cuban soldiers escorted Dixon away, and the plane, crew, and all passengers returned to Miami the same day.

A little more than four years later, five-year police veteran Michael McAllister, 39, and a backup officer arrived at the edge of South Haven to investigate a report of gunfire in the area. At 2:45 a.m., in the midst of a January 9, 1976, snowstorm, McAllister spotted a suspicious-looking man walking down the street and ordered him to stop. As McAllister, without the bulletproof vest he normally wore while on patrol, approached, the stranger suddenly turned and fired two shots from an automatic pistol into McAllister's abdomen and heart, killing him. The man then also tried to shoot the backup officer, but, when his pistol jammed, he dropped the weapon and fled. Other officers followed the gunman's footprints through the freshly fallen snow and arrested him an hour later.

A routine identification check with the FBI came back with a flabbergasting message: the officer's killer was hijacker Richard Dixon.

Dixon, acting as his own attorney, was convicted of second-degree murder for the McAllister killing and also later convicted in federal court of hijacking and kidnapping. Dixon, one of the very few airline hijackers ever caught and convicted, never revealed how he got out of Cuba or what he was doing in South Haven.

THE BABY-SITTER

Oakland County
February 15, 1976 - March 22, 1977

The streets became eerily absent of children.

February 15, 1976 — Mark Stebbins, 12, left the Ferndale American Legion Hall to go home to watch television but never arrived. Four days later, his body was found neatly laid out in funereal position in a snowbank next to a Southfield office building. Rope marks on his hands and feet indicated that Mark's killer had tied him up before sodomizing then smothering him.

December 22, 1976 — After an argument with her mother, twelve-year-old Jill Robinson stormed out of her Royal Oak home and walked to a party store on Woodward Avenue. Four days later, her body was found on I-75 north of 16-Mile Road in Troy. Jill's killer had not sexually molested her before sending a single shotgun blast into her head. Again, the killer had carefully placed the body in the snow.

January 2, 1977 — Kristine Mihelich, 10, left her home in Berkley and walked three blocks to a party store to buy a teen magazine. She didn't return home, and a mailman found her body nineteen days later in Franklin Village. Like the others, the killer had bathed Kristine and manicured her fingernails before smothering her and carefully laying out her body in a snowbank.

Ripples of apprehension flowed through Detroit's affluent northern suburbs. The bizarre and baffling murders, all of which began or ended in Oakland County, appeared to be the work of one deranged person. The ripples turned to waves of fear as investigators from several police departments in the thirteen-community area organized a task force and began a hunt for the killer they macabrely tagged "the baby-sitter" because of the great care and attention he lavished on his victims.

March 16, 1977 - Timothy King, 12, borrowed 30 cents from his older sister and, with his ever-present orange skateboard in hand, left his Birmingham home and walked to a drugstore five blocks away. After buying three candy bars, Timmy left through the store's rear door, which opened onto a parking lot, and disappeared. The police organized a dragnet involving more than three hundred local, county, and state officers and unsuccessfully searched for the boy for six days. In an impassioned television appeal, Tim's father begged the abductor to release his son, and Tim's mother placed a letter in the newspaper asking the kidnapper to let her boy come home so she could cook him his favorite meal, fried chicken.

On March 22, Timmy's body, dressed in freshly laundered and pressed blue pants and red jacket, was found gently laid out in a ditch along a rural Livonia road. The "baby-sitter" had carefully placed Timmy's orange skateboard near his body. Like Mark Stebbins, Timmy had been bound with rope at some point during his captivity and had been sexually assaulted. And, as a final act of either care or cruelty, the "baby-sitter" had fed Timmy a meal of fried chicken before smothering him.

Timothy King's murder left no doubt that the same deadly psychopath had committed all four ritualistic slayings, and a tidal wave of numbing shock and panic surged through Oakland County. Streets became eerily absent of children as parents, in a traffic-choking procession of vehicles, brought their children to and from school. Bicycles no longer lined up outside favorite sub-teen hangouts, and children even avoided playing in a park behind the Birmingham police station. Policemen, psychologists, and social workers visited nearly every elementary classroom in the thirteen-community area with instructions on what to do if approached by a friendly stranger. Schools called home to verify absences, and parents called schools if their children were late coming home. The few children who did walk to and from school were carefully watched by parents stationed along the routes. Place mats at a fast food restaurant, milk cartons in a supermarket, T-shirts, and bumper stickers all featured "don't talk to stranger" warnings, and the State Police, City of Birmingham, and *Detroit News* posted a $100,000 reward for information leading to the "baby-sitter's" capture.

The fear sometimes bordered on hysteria. Royal Oak police responded, en masse, to a call that "a girl is being abducted." The abductor turned out to be a father who had come to take his reluctant daughter home from a hamburger stand. And, at a Berkley elementary school, an angry mob surrounded a father who was trying to persuade his son to get into the family car for an unwanted trip to the dentist.

Also following Timothy King's murder, the police task force expanded its efforts and manpower to the point that their investigation became the most intensive manhunt ever conducted in Michigan. Operating under a $600,000 federal grant, the force, at its peak, included nearly two hundred full-time investigators, detectives, and civilian workers from eighteen police agencies. A surge of tips from people in all fifty states quickly overloaded the capacity of a donated computer, and the task force bought its own with $194,000 of state money. The force interviewed a half dozen people under hypnosis and even called in a New York psychic and a university team specializing in cult murders.

The task force uncovered a host of other crimes, and fifty spin-off investigations resulted in twenty arrests including:

— A father who "rented" his son to sexual deviates.

— A homosexual Boy Scout leader who had molested several boys in his troop.

— A fifteen-year-old male prostitute whose clients included several wealthy suburban businessmen.

— Members of a five-state child pornography ring.

But, after two years and 18,000 tips, the "baby-sitter's" identity still remained a mystery, and, on December 15, 1978, the task force officially ended its investigation. The "baby-sitter" never struck again, and police believe he is either dead or in prison.

A FIRE UNDER THE FOG

Dansville
March 9, 1977

As the years went by, Francine's fear turned to terror as each out-break of Mickey's violence brought her closer to death.

James "Mickey" Hughes threw his thirteenth beer can onto the living room floor as his wife Francine and three of their four children walked into their Dansville home. After finishing her secretarial courses at the Lansing Business College that day, Francine had gone to the grocery store and picked up some TV dinners the children had requested as a special, out-of-the-ordinary treat. As Francine put away the groceries, Mickey reached into the bag, pulled out the TV dinners, hit her in the mouth, and yelled, "You no good slut. We're not going to eat this s---." Turning to the shocked children he screamed, "You goddamned kids get out of here.'

Mickey then roughly grabbed his wife by the arm, dragged her into the living room, shoved her onto the couch and said coldly, "And another thing, bitch, I've made up my mind you're quitting school."

"I don't care what you do," Francine screamed with uncharacteristic defiance and independence. "I'm still goin'. If I have black eyes I'll go in. If I have to limp, I'll go in. You can't stop me."

"Oh, yeah," said Mickey as he ripped her school textbooks and notebooks to shreds and threw the crumpled pages into a heap. Then grabbing Francine by the throat, he demanded, "Now take this s--- out to the trash barrel and burn it or I'll break your f----- neck." Tears of pain and frustration stung Francine's puffed lips and her head throbbed as she carried weeks of schoolwork to the trash barrel and lit a match. A wisp of smoke rose, and she turned and went back into the kitchen.

Mickey called her into the living room. "*Now* are you going to quit school?" he sarcastically asked. But Francine, knowing that school was the only possible hope, the only remaining way out of her brutal, dehumanizing marriage, calmly replied, "No, Mickey. I'm not going to quit school. Mickey leaped from his chair, threw his beer all over Francine, and punched her viciously while screaming, "I'm going to kill you this time. You'd better say your prayers."

"Christy, call the police," Francine frantically yelled to her twelve-year-old daughter. As Christy raced across the yard to her grandmother's, Mickey's mother's, house, Mickey opened another beer and sat in his chair. After countless such beatings and calls he knew better than to let the police see him hit Francine. Twenty minutes later the police arrived, glanced at bruised and beer-soaked Francine, and asked Mickey, "Have you been hitting your wife?'

"Yeah, so what?" Mickey replied belligerently. "And what's more, I'm gonna kill her." Mickey wasn't drunk enough to swing at the police as he had done several times before, so the officers just told him to settle down and quit the foolish threats, then left.

Mickey stayed in his chair as Francine set the kitchen table and put the TV dinners and milk in front of the children. Francine tried to eat, but she couldn't put any food between her cut and swollen lips. Mickey came into the kitchen to get another beer, looked at the table, screamed, "I said we're not going to eat this s---," and dumped the table and contents onto the floor. He screamed at the kids to get up to their rooms as he grabbed Francine by the hair and pushed her down on her knees until her face almost touched the mess on the floor. "Now, bitch, clean it up," he demanded and sauntered out of the room.

Francine had just put the last of the garbage into a can when Mickey reentered the room, picked up the can, and dumped the mess onto the floor again. "Clean it up again," he said as he picked up a handful of garbage and rubbed it into her hair. "Now, bitch, do you still think you're going to go to school?"

Francine finally broke and sobbed, "No, Mickey, I'm not gonna go to school."

Not satisfied Mickey demanded, "Say it three times, whore."

"I'm not gonna go to school. I'm not gonna . . . I'm not gonna."

"Good," said Mickey, "now clean up this mess and, when you're done, make me something good to eat." Francine fixed Mickey's supper, brought it to him on a tray in the bedroom where he lay on the bed watching television, and returned to the kitchen to finish cleaning up.

After about fifteen peaceful moments, Mickey's voice rang out from the bedroom, "Francine, come here." As Francine entered the bedroom, Mickey grinned and said, "How about a little?" as he shoved her down on the bed.

At age twenty-nine, Francine Hughes had already endured nearly thirteen years of such degradation, humiliation, beatings, and domination. In 1965, convinced that

Mickey loved her deeply, and guilty because they had engaged in premarital sex, Francine, at age 16, consented to marry Mickey. Within six months, he beat her for the first time, and a pattern of beatings developed. Francine would do something — buy nail polish, visit a friend, or make a phone call — without asking Mickey's permission, and he would beat her. Francine's touchy, arbitrary, jealous, and intensely selfish husband dominated her life, and she became a tortured, powerless prisoner in her own home.

As the years went by, Francine's fear turned to terror as each outbreak of Mickey's violence brought her closer to death. Mickey beat, choked, and threatened Francine with knives. Police were called several times, and they arrested Hughes, more than once, not for beating Francine but for assaulting the police. Francine's in-laws and own family didn't want to be bothered with her problem, and most friends and neighbors pretended nothing out of the ordinary was happening. Occasionally, Francine reluctantly sought outside help, but police, social agencies, courts, and prosecuting attorneys either blandly turned aside her pleas or shuffled her to another unresponsive agency.

But finally, in 1971, Francine, broke, without food, behind in her rent, and pregnant, walked into the Legal Aid office. At their recommendation and with their help, she obtained a divorce from Mickey so that she could obtain welfare.

But, shortly after the divorce, Mickey was involved in a near-fatal automobile accident, and Francine, excessively compassionate and guilt-ridden, allowed him to move back in with her. As Mickey recovered, the beatings resumed, and he would not leave. "And if you try to leave," Mickey warned Francine, "I'll follow you wherever you go and kill you."

Francine determined that the only possible way out was to learn a skill. In spite of Mickey's taunts and constant interference, Francine finished high school by earning her General Equivalency Diploma and, in September, 1976, enrolled in a secretarial course at the Lansing Business College. Francine confided to her children that, in the spring when she got her diploma, things would be different.

But the words, "I'm not gonna go to school" and the memory of the fumes curling and blackening the edges of her books and papers stabbed at Francine's fragile spirit as Mickey, having animalistically gratified himself, turned over and went to sleep. Francine washed, got dressed, and told her frightened children they could safely come downstairs.

Francine paced nervously around the house, then suddenly blurted out to the children, "We're going to leave. I don't know where but we can't live like this anymore." She then bundled up the children, brought them to the car, and said, "Don't come back into the house. I'll be right back."

At 8:30 p.m., March 9, 1977, Francine reentered her home, picked up a gas can, unscrewed the lid, and went into the bedroom where her husband slept. She hesitated for a few seconds, sloshed gasoline around Mickey's bed, stepped just outside the room, put the can down, and struck a match. As Francine stuck the match into the bedroom, the fumes of gas caught with a roar, a rush of air slammed the door, and she screamed, "Oh, my God, what am I doing?"

Francine ran to her car, started it, and, as she and the

children drove away, looked back at the flames shooting out of the bedroom window. Francine drove to the Ingham County Sheriff's Department and sobbed hysterically, "I burned him up. I burned him up."

When fire fighters arrived at Francine's white house, clouds of dense dark smoke billowed from the windows, and, inside, Mickey Hughes lay dead of smoke inhalation.

The Ingham County Prosecutor charged Francine with first-degree premeditated murder, and her trial was set for October 15, 1977. Feminist groups, hoping to make her case a landmark for the rights of women beaten by their husbands, rallied to her defense. A legal system that fails to protect battered wives from their husbands, they claimed, drove Francine Hughes to the extreme action.

The trial only took seven days, and the jury deliberated only 6½ hours before finding Francine Hughes not guilty of murder by reason of temporary insanity. Said the jury foreman, "Most of us realized (Mrs. Hughes) was not in the right state of mind. Most of us just realized what she went through — what horrible circumstances she lived under." The trial judge said the verdict sent a signal to the world that thousands of battered women "are crying for help" and that the impact may be to "turn up a little fire under this fog . . ."

Less than two weeks after the jury found her innocent, doctors at the Center for Forensic Psychiatry at Ypsilanti interviewed her and pronounced her sane. Francine Hughes was finally free.

A PUNISHING SENTENCE
Ionia
April 25, 1978

Shortly after President Jimmy Carter was inaugurated, in 1976, as the nation's thirty-ninth president, Ira Randall Patton urged him, in a letter, to institute a nationwide death penalty for murderers. Wrote the Ionia man, "I believe it is a far better method than dying one day at a time in a prison and more humane."

On April 25, 1978, a jury convicted Patton of first-degree murder in the death of his estranged wife.

ABSTAIN FROM BLOOD
Detroit
July 12, 1980

It was not a duel, said the judge, since the two men had not previously arranged to shoot at each other.

In an east side Detroit neighborhood on July 12, 1980, 33-year-old Charles Williams cleaned paintbrushes in his grandfather's garage, unaware that, a half block away, two young men argued loudly in the street. Suddenly, one of the quarrelers yelled, "I'm going to get a gun," and both men dashed to their houses, grabbed guns, and blazed away at each other from opposite sides of the street.

As Williams wiped a brush, a stray bullet from the shoot-out whizzed into the garage, passed through his shoulder, and severed an artery near his lungs. The profusely bleeding Williams, a former Baptist turned Jehovah's Witness, was rushed to the hospital. But Williams refused a life-saving transfusion because his religion, based on a Bible verse that commanded, ". . . abstain from . . . blood," forbid it. Doctors operated to repair Williams' damaged blood vessel, but he died six hours later of heart failure from lack of oxygen caused by his heavy bleeding.

Prosecuting attorneys, using an 1848 Michigan anti-dueling statute that says anyone who "fights a duel . . . and in so doing shall inflict a mortal wound on any person" shall be charged with premeditated murder, arrested the man who fired the fatal shot and charged him with first-degree murder. But, two months later, a judge dismissed the first-degree murder charge because the seldom-used, anti-dueling law also stipulated that there must be a "previous appointment" to duel. The defendant, said the judge, had not previously arranged to shoot at his neighbor so the charges were reduced to second-degree murder.

But, argued the defense attorney during a week-long trial, the shooting wasn't murder at all since Williams caused his own death by refusing a transfusion. His argument was backed by the doctor who operated on Williams

who said that he was "90% certain" Williams would have
lived had he accepted a transfusion.

On July 31, 1981, a jury found the defendant guilty of
the greatly reduced charges of reckless and dangerous use
of a firearm and felonious assault and he was sentenced to
four years in prison.

THE REUNION

Farwell
February 16, 1982

*Helen locked the truck's doors and threw herself protectively over
her children.*

Fifty-three-year-old George Post and his 42-year-old
wife Vaudrey looked forward to hosting an informal
family reunion at their white, frame ranch house on Rock
Road in rural Farwell. Garnetta Haggart, Vaudrey's
23-year-old daughter from a previous marriage, had
flown in on February 15, 1982, for her final divorce proceedings, and the many local members of the large, close-
knit family had planned a February 16th get-together to
wish her well and re-acquaint her with her nieces and

nephews.

A year earlier, Garnetta had married Robert Lee Haggart, a 31-year-old high school dropout, Vietnam veteran, ex-convict, and livestock auctioneer from nearby Rosebush. Five short months after the wedding, Robert was charged with passing $17,000 worth of bad checks, and, when he left for Tennessee, Garnetta filed for divorce and moved to Florida. Garnetta planned to return to Florida immediately after her February 17th court appearance, so her extended family planned to make the most of the brief reunion.

But unknown to the family, an uninvited, deadly guest also planned to visit the Posts' farmhouse. On February 14, 1982, Robert Lee Haggart told a Tennessee friend that he had to "take care of some business" and boarded a Greyhound bus for Michigan.

During the early evening of February 16, members of the Post family, unaware that a murderous intruder lurked in the basement, began arriving at the house. George Post, a mail carrier, arrived home from work about 5:30 p.m. A few minutes later, a gray pickup truck filled with four chattering young children pulled into the yard. Twenty-nine-year-old Helen Gaffney, George's daughter by a previous marriage, and her children — Angela, 10, Tommy, 8, Amy, 4, and Amada, 1 — had arrived. Helen put away groceries, George arranged furniture, and the children played with coloring books while waiting for the other reunion guests to arrive.

At about 6:30 p.m., George Post went down to the basement recreation room to set up a card table and chairs. As he reached the bottom of the stairs, a twenty-gauge shotgun roared from six feet away and tore a hole through his chest, killing him instantly.

At the sound of the blast, Helen grabbed tiny Amanda in her arms, and, as the killer stepped over Post's body and climbed the basement stairs, Helen and her children ran coatless into the cold to their gray pickup truck. Nearly paralyzed with terror, Helen desperately reached for the ignition keys, but they were in her purse in the house. As the killer walked toward the truck, Helen locked the doors and threw herself protectively over her children. The gunman then fired a shotgun blast that shattered through the truck window and ended Helen's life. The murderer then killed Tommy with another round from the shotgun and, with a .38 caliber pistol, shot Angela and Amy once each through the head. As Amanda squirmed beneath the bloody bodies, the killer sent a final shotgun blast smashing through the other truck window at the baby. As the skies darkened, the slayer opened the truck door, covered the victims with an afghan, heaped snow on a pool of blood that ran out of the vehicle's open door, and returned to the house.

Several minutes later, Vaudrey Post and Garnetta Haggart returned from a shopping trip and entered the kitchen. The shotgun roared twice, and mother and daughter died together.

At 7:35 p.m., another Post daughter arrived for the family gathering. "Is anybody home," she called as she opened the door to the dark kitchen. She saw two dark shapes on the floor, snapped on the light, and recoiled in horror at the sight of her mother's and sister's blood-spattered bodies. She fumbled numbly for the kitchen phone, but it had been ripped out of the wall. So the Posts' shocked daughter and her husband, without noticing the bullet-ridden truck, hurriedly backed out of the driveway, sped to a neighbor's house, and called the sheriff's office.

At 8 p.m., the first deputy arrived, and, before the officer entered the house, he heard a soft moaning sound coming from the pickup truck. The deputy peered through the shattered truck window and saw a small foot wriggling beneath several bloody bodies. Amanda, unhurt but nearly frozen, covered with blood, and whimpering on the floor under the pickup's dashboard, had survived the third worst mass murder in Michigan's history.*

By 10 p.m., investigators determined that Vaudrey Post's light-blue, 1980 Buick was missing and posted a nationwide alert for the car. Investigators also talked to witnesses who reported seeing a short, stocky man with a very bushy beard in the vicinity of the Post house shortly before the shootings. Their description exactly fit Garnetta's estranged husband, Robert Lee Haggart, and, at 11:30 p.m., a nationwide bulletin was issued for his arrest.

On February 18, two days after the mass killings, Haggart, driving Vaudrey Post's Buick, was captured and arrested near the Tennessee-Alabama border. The arresting officers found, under the front seat, the .38 caliber pistol — two empty shells still in the chamber — that had been used to kill Angela and Amy.

Haggart was brought back to Michigan and tried. The prosecuting attorney called more than sixty witnesses and introduced two hundred exhibits, including a pair of Haggart's jeans and boots stained with an extremely rare

---

*The worst was the 1927 bombing of the Bath school (see p. 143). The second worst occurred in Detroit on July 14, 1971, when eight people were murdered in a Detroit "dope pad." The drug-related murders were never solved.

type of blood that matched two of the victims'. Haggart's defense attorney, on the other hand, called no witnesses and didn't put Haggart on the stand. The prosecution had established no motive, he argued, and had proved only that Haggart was at the murder scene and was driving a car belonging to one of the victims. But, at the conclusion of the month-long trial, the jury of six men and six women found Haggart guilty of six counts of first-degree murder and one count of second-degree murder.

On October 22, 1982, a Midland Circuit Court judge sentenced Haggart to seven life terms without parole for the murders, thirty to fifty years for the attempted murder of Amanda, and eight two-year sentences for using a firearm while committing a felony. The judge, who compared the killings to "the crimes of Buchenwald, Guyana, and West Beirut," expressed his own "revulsion and horror" at the murders saying, "You have again proven that civilization is a veneer and that there still lurks in the breast of a very few men the beastiality of Attila the Hun."

INDEX

217

Saginaw 42, 68, 140
Saginaw Valley 56, 67, 68, 89, 92
St. Anne's Church 18
St. Clair 195
St. Clair County 38
St. Clair River 24
St. Ignace 12-16, 20, 108
St. Joseph 33, 34, 63
St. Mary's River 11
Sanilac County 38
Sault Ste. Marie 7, 8, 13, 14, 17, 20, 49,
    55-58
Scalping 6, 26, 38
Schmidt, Herman 134-137
Schoolcraft County 108, 109
Schoolcraft, Henry Rowe 56, 57
Schoolcraft, James 55, 57, 58
Scott, George C. 173
Seneca 24
Seney 106, 108, 109
Seul Choix Point 70, 71
Seven-Mile Point 5
Shiawassee County 38, 110
Shooting 13, 16, 18, 19, 25, 35, 36, 47,
    58, 61-63, 72, 75, 80, 83, 87, 88, 94,
    97, 103, 105-108, 110, 117, 129,
    138, 142, 149-151, 153, 155, 157,
    158, 160, 165, 167, 169, 172,
    177-185, 187, 188, 190, 196, 197,
    208, 210, 211
Sigler, Kim 166, 167
Simmons, Stephen G. 44-46
Sims, Richard 180
Skyjacking 195, 196
Smith, Alphonso 179
Smith, Byron 191
Smith, Carl 180
Smith, E.C. 122, 123
Smothering (see also *Strangling*) 197, 198
Southern Michigan Prison (see also
    Jackson Prison and *Michigan State
    Prison*) 186
Southfield 197
South Haven 195, 196
Spain 67
Sparling, Albert 124-126
Sparling, Carrie 124-127
Sparling, John Wesley 124, 125
Sparling, Peter 124, 125
Sparling, Scyrel 126
Springfield Township 122
Springport 166, 167

Stabbing 3, 6, 18, 28, 31, 33, 39, 41, 49,
    94, 183, 185, 188
Stebbins, Mark 197-198
Steinbach, Augusta 134, 135, 137
Stewart, James 173
Straits of Mackinac 1-3, 12, 106
Strang, (King) James Jesse 62-64
Strangling (see also *Smothering*) 136,
    171, 185
Strikes, labor 129-133
Suicide 43, 113, 137
Sullivan, William 110-114
Sutker, Joseph 153
Sweet, Dr. Ossian 140-142
Sydnor, Jack 181

T

Talbert, George 183
Tanian, Philip 191
Tanner, Frank 180
Tanner, John 55-58
Tempe, Fred 182
Tennessee 210, 212
Terrell, Johnson 66
"Three Fires" 1, 2
Thurber, Dr. Frank 102, 103
Tilden, Bryant P. 57, 58
Tittabawassee River 160
Traver, Robert 172, 173
Treaty of Ghent 35
Trout Lake 108
Troy 197

U

Ubly 125
United Brotherhood of America (see
    Black Legion)
University of Michigan 126, 185
Upper Peninsula 2, 13, 59, 62, 64, 92,
    98, 106

V

VanWoert, Isaac 50-55
Vicksburg 47
Vienna, Austria 140
Vietnam War 210

Virginia 10, 28, 67, 68
Voelker, J.D. 172, 173
Voree, Wisconsin 62

W

Wadhams 36
War of 1812 33-37, 42
War of Independence 29
Washington, D.C. 67, 140
Washtenaw County 38, 51
Wayne 44
Wayne County 38, 45
Wentworth, Alexander 63, 64
Wesner, Conrad 47-49
West Beirut 213
Western Federation of Miners 129, 134
Wilberforce Academy 140
Williams, Charles 207-209
Williams, Fred 178
Williams, Perry 181
Williams, Prince 177
Wisconsin 5, 38, 62
Wolfe, General James 21
Wolverine Republican League 157
Woodstock Township 78
Woodworth, Benjamin 5, 46
World War I 133
World War II 163, 168, 172
Wright, Charles T. 101-104
Wurtemburg 82

Y

Young, Brigham 62
Young, Coleman 191
Ypsilanti 7, 99, 185, 186, 194, 206

Gary W. Barfknecht is a free-lance writer and director of amateur hockey programming. He, his wife Ann, and their two daughters, Amy and Heidi, live in Davison, Michigan.

Mr. Barfknecht's previous publishing credits include: *Michillaneous* (Friede Publications, 1982), *33 Hikes From Flint* (Friede Publications, 1975), *A Father, A Son, And A Three Mile Run* (Zondervan, 1974), and articles in the *Reader's Digest, Science Digest, Lion, Sign, Science & Mechanics, Lutheran Standard, Modern Maturity,* and other magazines.